Renée Harmon, a professional actress, scriptwriter, producer, and president of her own film production company, also lectures on film production at several California colleges.

PRENTICE-HALL INTERNATIONAL, INC., *London*
PRENTICE-HALL OF AUSTRALIA PTY. LIMITED, *Sydney*
PRENTICE-HALL CANADA INC., *Toronto*
PRENTICE-HALL OF INDIA PRIVATE LIMITED, *New Delhi*
PRENTICE-HALL OF JAPAN, INC., *Tokyo*
PRENTICE-HALL OF SOUTHEAST ASIA PTE. LTD., *Singapore*
WHITEHALL BOOKS LIMITED, *Wellington, New Zealand*
EDITORA PRENTICE-HALL DO BRASIL LTDA., *Rio de Janeiro*

THE
ACTOR'S
SURVIVAL GUIDE
FOR TODAY'S
FILM INDUSTRY

RENEE HARMON

A SPECTRUM BOOK

Prentice-Hall, Inc., Englewood Cliffs, New Jersey 07632

Library of Congress Cataloging in Publication Data

Harmon, Renée.
　The actor's survival guide for today's film industry.

　"A Spectrum Book."
　Includes index.
　1. Moving-picture acting—Vocational guidance.
2. Acting for television—Vocational guidance.　　I. Title.
PN1995.9.P75H37　1984　　　791.43'028'02373　　　83-11053
ISBN 0-13-003988-8
ISBN 0-13-003970-5 (pbk.)

1　2　3　4　5　6　7　8　9　10

ISBN 0-13-003988-8

ISBN 0-13-003970-5 {PBK.}

Editorial/production supervision by Chris McMorrow
Cover design © 1984 by Jeannette Jacobs
Manufacturing buyers: Christine Johnston and Edward J. Ellis

CONTENTS

PREFACE

This book has been written for you, the aspiring actor who wishes to make a career in the fascinating media of film, television, and commercials. It has been written for those of you who are actors already well on your way to your goal but who are continuing to encounter some hurdles. And it has been written for you the acting coach, whose task it is to guide your students away from the dreams of "fame and fortune" to the reality of achievable success. *The Actor's Survival Guide for Today's Film Industry* is your manual that advises you, step by step, on how to get started, how to succeed, and how to survive in this highly rewarding and exciting industry of ours. You'll find instructions that will lead you from the basics of the acting profession, such as how to find the right agent, how to join a union, how to write a successful résumé, and how to identify the kinds of headshot that will stimulate interest in you, to insights into effective preparation for interviews and auditions, and guidelines for a better understanding of the actor's emotional strengths and weaknesses.

    This book tells you frankly what it takes to become a professional screen actor. The film industry is a highly competitive and commercially oriented business. In order to be successful you must learn to adapt to its requirements. It is not easy for the actor coming from a college drama department or community theater environment to view his or her acting ability not as a God-given art but as a craft that has to be developed and disciplined along certain lines. For this very reason, *The Actor's Survival Guide for Today's Film Industry* makes you realize your *commercial identity*.

Yet, the guide goes further. Unlike many other admittedly good books, it does not restrict itself to the surface basic facts of getting started in this business. You will be advised on what kinds of classes and workshops to choose from; and you will also learn about interview techniques and how and where to hunt for your first acting jobs. All these points are covered thoroughly and clearly.

But the *Guide* is *special*. It is the first book of its kind to explore the fact that, in the final analysis, it is you the actor who holds the key to final success. You will be guided to gauge your own success potential carefully. Your eyes will be opened to your hidden assets, the ones you never thought to exploit, and most important, you will become acquainted with the facts that might keep you from reaching your full artistic and human potential.

Most significantly, this book reveals the *secret of the successful screen actor:* the process of building a *unique personality* and the final projection of it on screen.

The *Guide* aims to be your mentor, a good friend that wants to help whenever you need advice. I myself am an actress as well as a motion picture producer and therefore have had the chance to meet both with many actors already active in the industry and with aspiring actors whom I have the opportunity to observe during college seminars that I teach. The information given in the *Guide* is based on firsthand knowledge of the demands of the film industry. I hope that this book will make the brass ring of success a little bit easier to catch for all of you.

Good luck.

THE
ACTOR'S
SURVIVAL GUIDE
FOR TODAY'S
FILM INDUSTRY

WHERE
TO FIND JOBS
IN THE
FILM INDUSTRY

Before you make the commitment to become a professional actor and embark on this long road that slowly winds its way to success, you should consider the long years that must be spent in preparation as well as the money that will have to be expended on acting classes, pictures, wardrobe, and the like. You must also consider the fact that it is almost essential for you to live in New York or Los Angeles in order to further your career. Certainly you can spend many years at home or anywhere there is a good drama department at your local college or a reputable acting school. You can also "wet your feet" with performances at community theaters, but eventually the road will lead you to Los Angeles or New York if you are at all serious in your desire to become a professional actor.

You should further consider the work possibilities the acting profession will offer you and the financial rewards you might receive. After all, you do have to eat, and unless you were born with the proverbial silver spoon in your mouth, you must provide for certain necessities. Everyone knows of the fabulous salaries that movie stars make; we have all seen pictures of their magnificent homes; we have all heard about the "unknowns" who earn between $1,500 to $2,500 a week on TV series, with a guarantee of thirteen weeks; and we are all familiar with the fact that the day-player SAG-minimum scale* is going up every few years. So we say to

*SAG minimum applies to the minimal amount actors get per day or week. These amounts are determined by the Screen Actors Guild, a nationwide actors' union. The scale amount is open to negotiation every few years with the film and TV companies signatory with SAG. These companies abide by the rules set by SAG. These rules also cover working conditions and residuals for commercials and television shows.

ourselves, "Not bad at all. Even if I don't become a star, I can make a decent living in a career that I love."

Granted, it looks very good. It looks even better as we take a look at the money that is paid to superstars in almost limitless amounts. Even "run of the mill" names make from $100,000 to $200,000 a picture, and the big stars of the long-running TV series earn well over a $1 million a year. Fantastic. Right, but now let's take a good hard look at the other side of the coin. The big monies are earned only by a few, but there are many many more who are members of the Screen Actors Guild in Hollywood and New York or members of AFTRA and an enormous number who belong to neither union.

The following is a short breakdown showing the income level of SAG actors during the past few years:

$100,000 and over	1%
$25,000–$35,000	2%
$15,000–$25,000	5%
$8,000–$15,000	6%
$5,000–$8,000	7%
$2,000–$5,000	9%
$1,000–$2,000	14%
$1,000 and under	56%

These figures do not apply to any given year but rather average the income over the span of several years (the percentile is taken on the averages). These figures include *all* income derived from screen appearances, including commercials. Even more depressing is the fact that after years of intensive study, the actor is only able to do one thing, *act.* True, acting is an overcrowded field, but at least in other fields that are overcrowded, such as law, a young attorney always has the opportunity to find employment in fields unrelated to law, because any employer is aware that this young person's education has given her or him tools that are applicable in a number of other positions.

The choices available to college graduates are generally very wide; that is to say, even if they don't find positions in their own field of study, they are employable in a number of other professions. But what can actors do besides act? Yes, they can teach, but if they desire to teach for a public school, they must have a B.A. degree with strong emphasis on education, because they will be required to teach other subjects as well as acting. If one considers a teaching position at a college, an M.A. in Drama is required.

The point is, should you choose acting as a full-time profession, you must have some other work to fall back on. Don't put all your eggs in one basket. Looking at the SAG income figures, you, too, will agree that you will need another job. Hopefully this will only hold true for the beginning of your acting career, but for many, far too many, SAG actors, their nine-to-five jobs support them all of their lives while they pursue acting. Keeping this in mind, you must realize that the job you choose to "tide you over till the big break comes," must be substantial enough to keep you from going hungry and be challenging enough for you to enjoy. Only if you can enjoy the job you have will you be able to go full force after your acting career. Only if you enjoy this job will you avoid the bitterness so many actors face while waiting to act.

Let's assume that after all of these bleak and discouraging thoughts, you still decide to pursue your acting career, giving it a try no matter what. You won't throw this book in the trash can or wrap it up for a birthday present for your cousin Betsy whom you never liked while you quickly make an appointment at your nearest employment center or look through your college catalog for a field of other endeavor. Let's assume that you decide to stick it out, because you are the one in thousands who has it and will make it. Good for you if nothing can discourage you.

First, let's take a closer look at where your employment possibilities lie. It could be a feature film, either at a major studio or an independently produced film; a television show; cable TV,* a commercial; or an industrial or educational film. A nice long list, as you can see. Now, let's scrutinize each field separately. Since usually in the beginning of your career you will derive most of your income from commercials, let's talk about commercials first.

COMMERCIALS

Commercials are the actor's bread and butter. Fifty percent of all commercials are produced in New York. Thirty percent of the commercials are produced in Los Angeles, the rest are made in large cities such as San Francisco, Atlanta, and Chicago. The salaries derived from a commercial that goes nationwide and runs on the air for a considerable amount of time can be fabulous.

If you are one of the actors in a nationwide commercial, you will laugh all the way to the bank as you deposit your residual checks. Residuals are the monies paid to an actor every time his or her commercial is aired on TV. Since not all commercials reach "the Big Time," that is to say nationwide airing, we will discuss the structure of commercials.

In the course of your career you may do a local commercial that

---

*The advice given and opinions expressed in the segment on television applies to cable TV as well.

shows in your hometown or a territorial commercial that shows in several states. If the commercial was non-union-made, you are not eligible to receive residuals. If you move up to a lucrative nationwide commercial, the case is different. Let's assume a fast food chain wants to shoot a new commercial. First they will produce several tests shooting various commercials, each one different in theme, or they might shoot several on the same theme. They will use several actors in sets for each one. These actors will work one to three days and most likely receive SAG-scale pay. Usually unknowns are used for commercials unless the sponsor demands a star or known name. Of the commercials then submitted by the production company, the sponsor, along with the advertising agency, will select between four to six commercials. These will be given a test run by being shown in various areas, such as southern California, the Midwest, and the Eastern Seaboard. They will run for several weeks, and all the actors who appear on screen will receive residuals every time the commercial is shown. The principal actors, those speaking lines or those featured principally, receive the residuals. Extras otherwise called *atmosphere actors,* are not eligible for this benefit. You can easily see how commercials can become very lucrative. The actors who worked in the commercials that were not chosen to air will receive only their scale pay. But this is how the industry works; you will get used to it. Of course, the possibility always exists that once a test commercial has been selected for nationwide airing, it may be reshot with known actors; then you will receive no residuals.

If a commercial is shot for a foreign company, American made but distributed in foreign countries *only,* then you are not entitled to residuals, but only the salary agreed upon. If this is the case, any good agent will try to get you twice the scale pay, since residuals will not be forthcoming no matter how long the commercial runs. Most foreign commercials are shot non-union and therefore can be a good opportunity for beginning actors to start their commercial careers. Some production companies shoot non-union commercials exclusively. For these non-union commercials, you will not receive residuals and usually a salary far below the scale pay. If you are a member of SAG, you cannot act in a non-union commercial.

Commercial Identity

Even if you are just starting out in your acting career, you will not have much difficulty getting a commercial agent to sign you if you are the *right commercial type.* You must have *commercial identity* in order to become a successful actor for commercials. Commercial identity is the look the purchasing public can identify with as you sell the product. If you look like the girl next door *would like to look like,* with flowing hair, bright smile, and shining eyes, or if you are handsome and athletic as the guy next door *would like to be,* or maybe your gray hair and kind, grandmotherly, understanding quality conveys itself to the woman watching the TV and wishes her own mother had always looked upon her like you do, then you have commercial identity. If your confidence inspires others to wish you were their doctor or attorney, then you have the commercial look.

Commercials work on the audience's subconscious, and a woman watching a shampoo commercial is not watching the bottle of shampoo per se but the beautiful model displaying the shampoo. As she watches, she establishes, unknown to herself, a relationship with the model and puts herself into the model's place, feeling that her hair will bounce and shine as luxuriously as the model's if she buys the same shampoo the model uses. She knows full well that her hair will never look like the model's tresses, but a subconscious symbiotic relationship has been established, and as she walks along the aisle of her favorite drugstore, there is a good chance she will recognize the shampoo that was "pushed" by the commercial and be tempted to give it a try. At this point we seem to be faced with the obvious contradiction that while the advertising firm is selling a product, they are really selling you, the "type," the commercial identity, since you symbolize the benefit the product will bestow upon the buyer.

Let's take another example of the suggestive control of commercials. Think about either a boat or a car commercial. Have you ever noticed that the luxury boats and cars are never advertised with a family of four plus luggage and pet dog piling into the contraption? No, there is always a beautiful model floating up to the boat or car, suggesting to you that if you buy this product, the beautiful woman will come with it. Now, quickly look into a mirror and establish your commercial type.

Who Will Make It in Commercials?

Eighteen to twenty-three is the best age to be successful in commercials, provided you have a wholesome American look. If you are over this age yet look fifteen or sixteen, then you've got it made. You will be in demand, because any production company will hire you before they will hire a real sixteen-year-old actor. The reason for this is that according to SAG rules, you are an adult and can work full-time, while the sixteen-year-old is still considered a child actor. There are very stringent labor rules concerning child actors.

If you are young, you will have a few prosperous years, but if you fail to make the transition from ingenue to leading lady or juvenile to leading man, you may fall by the wayside. You may in those years get success from having the right look and bright smile alone, but as soon as the first youth is gone and a new crop of faces is available, those actors who are unable to make the transition may find themselves out of work. This is a sad, cruel fact of life. Certainly a woman in her middle twenties can look sensational, but in comparison with an eighteen-year-old actress, she lacks one of the most precious commercial commodities, *youth*.

However, she should not get discouraged. The fact that she is a little older doesn't necessarily mean she will have a less rewarding acting career, although now that she is older, she must have *training*. The days are gone when all she had to do was simply smile into the camera. Once the transition from youth to adult leads is made, the actor and actress have many good years ahead of them, since looks do not change so dramatically once you have celebrated your twenty-fifth birthday.

The middle years are the most difficult ones in which to break into commercials, especially for the beginning actor. Most leading ladies and leading men who are already well trained and have much experience behind them fall into the age group of thirty-five to forty-five. This makes your chances as a beginner slimmer. Let's assume you are a vivacious housewife whose children are in school or a salesman bursting with personality and you wish to try your hand at commercials, "for fun," and to earn a little money on the side. If you have no training and your last acting class was in high school or college, then your chances of getting a foothold in the field of commercials are not good. But don't give up, because you never know what may happen in this business.

If you want any measure of success, you must have *training*. Before even attempting to register in an "Acting for Commercials" class, you should develop a solid background in basic acting classes. Experience some classes in improvisational-acting workshops. Don't look for an agent until you have at least one year of intensive training under your belt, and if you have comedic ability, you would do well to strengthen it by attempting a comedy class taught by a professional comedian.

I know that the entire picture looks discouraging, but if after sufficient preparation you really want to give commercials a try, don't hesitate. Getting started will be hard. It might take you two or three times as long to find an agent as it would someone younger. You will be turned down many times, you will wait a long time from interview to interview, from job to job, but if you stick with it, you will make it. Also remember, time is on your side. Once you move from leading lady to character actress or from leading man to character actor, you have gained experience in the years in between and your chances of making a successful career of commercials are excellent.

I have seen a number of delightful senior citizens make a terrific second career in commercial acting after their retirement. The ones who were most successful were those who approached this risky career with a sense of adventure and fun. They did not have the burning desire to succeed like their younger counterparts. However, a word of warning: Don't depend on your looks or terrific commercial identity alone. You, too, must have a solid acting background, just like your friends in their middle years. You should have at least one year of intensive training in a good school or college acting class before you begin to send out your pictures and résumé.

I have seen instances where actors and actresses who had fabulous commercial identity signed with an agent practically at the snap of their fingers. Unfortunately, they never really had the kind of training one must have in order to survive in this highly competitive business. The problem that these actors and actresses encountered simply was that once they were submitted to an audition or interview, they did not deliver. Reading commercial copy, they were nervous, ill at ease, did not look at the camera, flubbed their lines; in short, they proved to be rank amateurs.

Children in Commercials

Children are the backbone of commercials, because there is always a demand for new faces. It is true that a child's career can be relatively short-lived as far as commercials are concerned. The prime years for children are between the ages of five and eleven, yet almost all agencies will accept babies from six months up to the teenager of seventeen years old. The thing about commercial children is that a youngster doesn't have to look cute or be especially pretty to have a good chance at being a commercial actor. The old look of the curly-haired and dimpled Shirley Temple is definitely out and hopefully gone for good. What is *in* is naturalness. Agents now want children who have the natural commercial identity of the freckle-faced "kid next door."

The prime requirement that a child must have today in order to become a successful commercial actor is personality spelled with a capital *P*. This personality must be outgoing. Shy or introverted children will not make it at all in commercials, no matter how talented or creative they may be. The children who agents want today must have vitality and liveliness as well as the ability to take direction quickly and easily. It is certainly not necessary and is in fact preferable if the child has absolutely *no* formal acting training at all. This is true especially of those in the age group from five to eleven years old. Older children, on the other hand, would do well to have some training, but the younger child is much more delightful if left alone. Acting training in this age group will only hamper the child's natural ability. A child who is forced to recite lines to become a character, in most cases alien to her or his own personality, is ruined for commercial acting in the process.

It is especially damaging when parents feel they are doing little Annie a favor by pushing her to perform in school plays where equally well-meaning directors and teachers squeeze the natural vitality out of her by making her "act the part." Yes, classes are good for Annie, but these classes could include dancing (tap or ballet), tumbling, and singing. Other classes might be ice skating, roller skating, or skiing, but never acting. The only activity where Annie might benefit is in an improvisational children's workshop taught by an experienced acting teacher.

Child actors are under very strict labor laws, which is as it should be. A child of six and under is permitted six hours on the set, and out of these the child is permitted to work only three hours. Children between the ages of six and seventeen can work only four hours a day and must have at least three hours of schooling plus one hour of recreation. A welfare worker must be provided for all performers under the age of seventeen, and anyone under the age of eighteen must be accompanied by a guardian.

It is fairly easy for an outgoing youngster to find an agency, but parents should be aware that it is better to have a child with an agency that specializes in child actors. If a child is with an agency that deals primarily with adults, the child may "stay on the shelf," because the commercial production companies might not contact this agency when they need to cast a child. Therefore, even if your own agent wants to represent your child, it is better to decline and go to one specializing in children. If you live some distance from the large cities, then the adult agency usually serves as a children's agency also.

Having a child who does commercials is a full-time job for the child's mother or father. It is *you* who has to drive your child to interviews, wait with your child to keep him or her amused. It is *you* who must drop whatever you are doing when the agent sets up an interview. You are the one who helps the child learn lines and who sits with him on the set or location in either hot or cold, and always drafty, studios while he is working. If you are a working mother, it is almost impossible to let your child do commercials. In this case, your child needs a *personal manager*. The personal manager doesn't guide your child's career, but is usually a woman with children of her own doing commercials as well as film and television. The personal manager takes children under her wing and drives them to commercials, interviews, rehearsals, and auditions and will be present while they are at work on the set. Personal managers' usual and well-deserved fee is 20 percent of your child's earnings. Personal managers will not negotiate for a new or better agent or for better contracts. They will not look for jobs for the children they represent. If you feel you would like a personal manager, call some reliable agents who deal with children for recommendations.

Be aware that the expenses encountered for a child actor are much heavier than for those of an adult. A child grows up very quickly, and you might have to go the photographer route for pictures twice a year. If your child is working quite steadily, she or he will miss out on many school and children's activities. If he works very little, he will have to face the rigors of rejection, an emotional experience that is hard enough on adults, but even harder on a child and may leave emotional scars.

If your child works fairly steadily, the rewards can be high. It is not uncommon that children earn enough for a college education while only working a few short years. Many children stop their acting career as soon as the "pickings get slim." There are others who go on and make exciting acting careers. Some of these have to face disappointment when the later years don't match their early promise of success. A few youngsters grow up into unhappy adults because of early exposure to acting, but most are happy and outgoing, facing the rigors of their working conditions with amazing stamina. Their attitude is a credit to them, as well as their parents, agents, and all the people they work with on the set.

TELEVISION

You have studied and worked hard, gotten a commercial agent, done one or two commercials, become a member of SAG, gotten a theatrical agent, and now you are up for your next step on the ladder of success, you are ready for television.

Television encompasses everything we see on the small screen. There are the giants, the big networks like NBC, CBS, and ABC. And there are independently owned stations all across the country airing syndicated shows. These shows may be series and shows that have already had their run on the big networks, or they may be produced especially for these independent stations. Often a film which has had a limited theatrical run finds an appreciative audience on television.

Basically we can divide television shows into the following categories:

Series (situation comedy and drama)

Movies made for television

Soap operas

In all these categories you will find the following structure of roles:

Star

Co-star

Featured

Bit (over five lines)

Bit (under five lines)

On the series you will find *regulars*. These are actors who are featured in almost every show. *Semi-regulars* are actors who are featured every so often. *Guest stars* are the actors of considerable stature who appear generally in one segment only.

The movies made for television and commissioned by the big networks fall within the realm of full-length feature films. They may have special effects, exciting car chases, and stunts that put many independent films to shame.

As we look at movies made for television, we should differentiate between the "made-for-TV movies" and the "movies of the week." A movie of the week runs ninety minutes, whereas made-for-TV movies run the traditional two hours. Some of these movies that are transferred from tape to film will be shown as theatrical features overseas.

In the television series we differentiate between situation comedies, called *sitcoms,* and dramatic shows. It is pretty difficult for a new actor to get cast for a sitcom, since these usually feature a permanent cast, some semi-regulars, and every so often a guest star, but the prospect looks brighter in drama. In comedy, the shows normally run thirty minutes, whereas in drama they run sixty minutes, which means that more actors are needed. Also in drama, a wide variety of actors are used, especially in the pure action shows. The prime requirements for these shows are that the actors project a *definite type* that fits the identity of teacher, policeman, doctor, or gangster. The acting should be simple and clear, and the emotions expressed believable.

Movies made for television are a good proving ground for the beginning actor, although you will seldom have the opportunity to read for a part of any importance, since the already experienced actors will usually take these parts. You should remember that the producers and sponsors have the right to demand *recognizable names*. If you consider the huge amounts of money spent on a television show, not only the cost of producing and advertising but especially the cost of buying air time, you can understand why they dare not risk unknowns, no matter how right for the part an actor may be.

In order to get your first reading chance, you should have a solid background of film experience. You might attend a *good* recognizable film acting school or be cast in a number of college-grad films.* Just having commercial experience will not get you very far in film.

*A *college-grad film* refers to a film shot by a candidate for a Master's Degree in lieu of a written thesis.

Most television series and films made for television are produced by the major studios, such as Warner, Universal, and Columbia. There are a few independent companies producing TV shows, but they are all very closely connected with a major studio. At the studios, television casting is separate from feature casting. Usually one casting director will cast features and another will cast television series.

Soap Operas

New York is still the center for most soap operas. A few soaps are produced in Los Angeles at CBS and NBC studios. Fortunately the soaps are very receptive to new actors, and they do keep their doors open for you. I may sound repetitive, but you must be skilled in order to be considered for a soap. Your acting must be subdued if you are to portray a supposed life situation believably. There is no place for histrionics on soaps. The entire concept of the soap rests on the close interaction of characters whom the audience is thoroughly familiar with. It is true that many people are so hooked on soaps that they feel the characters to be their own friends and enemies in whose fate they take a deep interest.

The workload on a soap is heavy. The day begins early in the morning. You rehearse with half-closed eyes. As you sip your first cup of coffee, you will be notified about any rewrites that have occurred. You will constantly have to deal with rewrites and changes, which take place during the rehearsal as you run through your scene several times. After the lunch break, you go to costuming and makeup. The actual shooting takes place in the afternoon and may last—well, until the show is in the "can." If you are scheduled to work the next day, you will have to learn the lines of the next day's script when you get home that night.

Soap actors are well paid and earn a lot of recognition. Some actors have moved on from soaps to stardom, which they highly deserve, believe me—they work very hard.

Soap operas come under AFTRA contracts. If you are a member of AFTRA, you can also work as an extra on an AFTRA show. Many AFTRA actors started out doing extra parts and moved up to bits of under five lines, then to bits of over five lines, and eventually to better roles.

FEATURE FILMS

Feature films come in various shapes and sizes. There are the big block busters produced by major studios that cost $30 to 40 million and take years to produce. There are the average films, whose budgets range from $5 to 10 million, and then there are the major studios' low-budget films, which can cost up to $4 million in production. Some larger independent companies produce multimillion-dollar films, but they are entwined with the major studios as far as releasing and distribution goes, so that for all practical purposes these big independents should be termed studio productions. The casting process for these films might take months, and there is little chance for a new actor to get cast in a major studio film. Even for the smaller parts the studio demands actors who have at least some stature and are represented by a well-known agency.

There are also a great many films of high technical and artistic calibre that are produced independently by some medium-sized companies and are financed through foreign monies. These films are American-produced but must be shot in the country of financing and use actors, personnel, crews, and labs in that particular country. These companies do not give money to the American filmmakers out of the goodness of their hearts but rather to boost their own film industry. The American production company is usually permitted to take either two American stars or one American star and one director on the project. Everyone else has to be hired in the country of financing.

As you can easily see from all these examples, there is very little chance for a beginning actor to be cast in either a foreign-financed or studio-financed project. Nevertheless, a new actor *should* and *will* find work in independent film companies.

Most films produced by small independent companies fall into the exploitation category. They are action films, karate films, and films of the horror genre. Some of these exploitation films are geared for the teenage group with titles such as *High School Party, Teenage Revenge,* and so on. The term *exploitation* doesn't apply to "girlies" or "nudies" or, even worse, straight pornography. Stay away from the "nudies" and soft-X-rated pictures that are so popular now that they sell like hotcakes for cable as well as home video. These movies won't help your career and might even curtail it for you. Granted, if you are young, pretty, and can act, you will be snapped up for a starring role, and you might even have a lucrative, although short-lived, career, but you will never have a lifelong career. No television show or reputable feature film company will hire you after you have been literally "exposed" in these films. Appearing in these films will end your career before you have even begun. True, there are a number of actresses who have made some sort of name for themselves in these films who had beauty, talent, and personality, but when they tried to get on the big screen or on television, in most cases they failed. Of course some feature films include nudity, but my feeling is that you should be very careful when considering and accepting such a part. Generally, nudity, no matter how well done or how tasteful, will not help your career if you are a beginner.

Fortunately for all actors there are a great number of low-budget films being produced every year. These films are not as highly touted as their major-studio counterparts, yet they are very much alive. You won't find *Beetles Out of Space* or *Iron Fists* in any of your main-chain first-run theaters, but films with such titles are healthily holding their own all over the country in small drive-in theaters and small hardtops, that is to say movie theaters that are considered third-run, showing major films after they have run their course in the bigger theaters.

Because of the relatively small number of release prints the independents can put on the market, which is about a hundred prints or less, in comparison with the thousands released by the majors, the small exploitation films have a much longer life span as they slowly creep their way across the United States from territory to territory. These films also have high sales rates all over the world and are in truth the "dyed in the wool" international films that flicker happily from Oklahoma to Libya and from Louisiana to Japan, Africa, and all throughout Southeast Asia. They are very much in demand in the overseas theatrical, as well as home-video, markets.

True, the plots of these pictures are simple, the production values leave much to be desired, and the acting and directing are not up to Academy Award–winning standards, but these are also the films that are so good to a new actor. These are the films that gave many of our stars, such as Jack Nicholson, their first start in pictures. Small independents are forced to let even considerable parts be played by relatively unknown but nevertheless well-trained and skilled actors. These companies usually cast one recognizable name for the lead, while the rest are unknown actors.

The money you can make on such small independent films is not great, because they will rarely pay you over SAG scale. These films usually have a shooting schedule of about three weeks. Your agent will notify you if you have an interview with such a small, but SAG-signatory* production company.

Going down the ladder a few steps, we arrive at the production companies that shoot non-union, that is to say, they are not signatory with SAG and therefore cannot hire union actors. Once you are a member of SAG, you cannot work for these companies, and if you do, you will be fined and may even lose your SAG membership. If you are in doubt as to whether or not the company for whom you are auditioning is SAG, simply call your local SAG office, ask for "Productions," and inquire whether the company in question is signatory. These non-union companies usually shoot on a very low budget. Technically speaking, they are not production companies but

*Any film or television production company who has signed an agreement with SAG is *signatory*. The agreement states that the company will abide by SAG regulations as far as pay, workman's compensation, and working conditions are concerned.

rather *filmmakers,* that is to say, the producer is also the director or cinematographer and will most likely edit the film, work on sound, and do all the special effects. In short, the brunt of the entire film will rest on the filmmaker's shoulders.

Assuming you are still non-union, you would do well to consider these small films. Your agent will not inform you of them, because they are not listed with the breakdown service,* but you may hear about them through friends or see them advertised in the trade papers, such as *Drama Log* in Los Angeles or *Back Stage* in New York.

The filmmakers who work on such small budgets are usually the true enthusiasts. They are people who live and breathe film. They are the ones who literally go hungry to squeeze out another week of editing-table rent, they work at jobs they dislike in order to save money for filmmaking. They really deserve the highest respect. Some of their output is of high artistic and technical quality, while some is just acceptable. These filmmakers are of quite a sizable number, and many bring out a film every two years or so. Even though the films get limited play dates foreign and domestically, they stay alive for several years, giving the actors who appear in them good exposure.

One unfortunate aspect of these non-union films is that often filmmakers cast months ahead of the projected shooting date and light-years ahead of the final financing. This practice is unfair to actors. If casting is to be done as carefully and artistically as it deserves, producers should give themselves about three months before the shooting date, but not before financing has been secured. Casting should not be done with financing still a nebulous undertaking, to be tackled somewhere in the future. So, if you are reading for a non-union independent, don't hold your breath. The wonderful leading role for which you were reading may never materialize.

Let's move ahead now and assume the filmmaker has secured his or her financing, the locations are set, the raw stock has been bought, the equipment has been rented, and the film is ready to roll. As you are called in to sign your contract, you might be asked to "go deferred." Many non-union productions hire their actors on *deferment.* This means you will be paid your salary sometime after the film is completed. Normally the contract will state, "Deferment upon net profit." This means you may have a very long wait before you see a penny. The first money received from domestic as well as foreign distribution goes for paying off the lab for answer prints and possibly release prints. Next, the investors will be paid off their initial investment, lately with a heavy interest rate tacked on. Hopefully if some

---

*The term *breakdown service* refers to a list available to agents. Producing companies list each show to be cast, giving a short synopsis of the story, then name, age, and personality traits of each character.

profits roll in, you will get paid. So, if you go on the terms "deferred upon net profit," make certain that the following clause is added: "Recoupment in first place with investors." This clause means that you will get your deferred payment at the same time that the investors collect their profits. Let me repeat, you will *not* see one penny unless the lab has been paid and the investors have recouped their original investment.

Many actors contend that the deferred-payment system is unfair. I happen to disagree. I realize that actors put their talent and their time on the line, but so does the filmmaker. Often filmmakers have their own money invested, and should the film never be released, they lose their investment completely. Actors, on the other hand, have at least some film on themselves and a credit to their advantage. If the film does get distributed they get exposure, a benefit the new actor cannot buy.

It is true that doing a non-union film is no picnic. The hours are long, about twelve to sixteen a day. The working conditions are often unbearable: You may be sweating in the heat and freezing in the cold. But the spirit on most of these shoots is fantastic. The excitement spreads to everyone, from the director to the gofer, because they all love film and they would rather shoot than do anything else, because now, finally, at this moment, everyone has a chance at the brass ring of success.

EDUCATIONAL
AND TRAINING FILMS

These films, even though non-union, are produced by highly reputable and professional firms. Most of them are either 16mm shorts or videotapes. They are made for schools and colleges or are ordered by manufacturing firms to train their employees. The U.S. Army and Navy have a highly developed production program for such training films. Because these films are nonunion, your agent will not be aware of any opportunity for you to work in them. You will have to rely on information you find in the trade papers* in Los Angeles or New York

There are many of these small companies scattered all across the United States in various towns and cities. You could check the Yellow Pages for the names of such companies or contact the audio-video department of your local college and ask for a list of the firms that supply the college with educational films or tapes. Then send them a picture and résumé to be placed on file. It is also a good policy to call them every now and again to inquire when they might begin a new project for casting or recasting.

Daily Variety, Hollywood Reporter, Back Stage, Drama Log, Casting Call.

The pay for these *industrials,* as the collective term goes, is very poor, but even though these films will not give you exposure, they will give you experience. Working on these films also looks good on your résumé and informs the casting director of the fact that you have worked in front of a camera.

PERSONALITY, YOUR WINNING CARD

It's not easy to become an actor, to remain an actor, or to stay in the business and show any degree of success. Acting is an extremely overcrowded profession.

As you start out on your career, you must look at the profession in a business sense. Many actors arrive in Los Angeles or New York, protected by the success they had achieved in college. They view acting as an art. True, acting should be and many times is art, but art is merely one consideration of this vast mass-media entertainment industry, of which you, the actor, are but one component.

TYPECASTING

Stage actors have been trained to stretch themselves so as to portray many diversified characters effectively. Such actors can depict teenagers as believably as they can old people, but as far as film and TV are concerned this skill is wasted, since they will only be cast for the *type* they *project*. The screen demands *reality*. The casting directors who cast feature film will allow for some creativity, but television casting directors demand and instantly recognize the type since a character has to be established quickly and clearly.

For instance, if a director has to cast an accountant, she or he will choose a smallish, meek-looking man who wears glasses. This is called *typecasting.* If you are an accountant but look like a quarterback, that's how you will be cast; forget ever being cast in the role of an accountant.

SAG has tens of thousands of members, and any casting director can get numerous representatives of any type he or she wishes. So, if your star performance in college was as seventy-year-old Aunt Lizzie, forget about it, because the casting director has access to many seventy-year-old actresses. One look at the Academy Players Directory* and you will agree with me. In the directory you will find the following categories:

MALE	FEMALE
Juvenile	Ingénue
Leading Man	Leading Lady
Character	Character

These rather loosely knit categories are primarily age groupings. Juvenile and Ingenue ranges between eighteen and twenty-five years old. You are a Leading Man and Leading Lady if you admit to being between twenty-four and forty years old, and after about forty-five you move into the ranks of the Character Actor. So you see, first you will be cast according to your age. This is easy. The next step, however, is a little more complicated, because you will have to be able to project a definite personality type to the viewer that will be instantly recognizable.

The reason why so many actors are vague in projecting a definite type is, first of all, that they cannot effectively project the person they really are. This is to say that they cannot project their *core personality,* which is the base upon which their specific type is rooted.

To be an effective type, you must first of all be *yourself.* At this early point in your career you should realize that every one of us is *unique.* No two of us are alike, and this is where your individual strength and appeal are based. Uniqueness is your biggest asset. Many actors are completely unaware of their vast source of power, some because they hide behind the sheltering facade of a phony personality tailored out of the many roles they have played, others because they work so hard to appear "laid back" that they seem bland and uninteresting. In both instances the actors obliterate their own personality.

In conclusion let me say that typecasting is nothing more nor less than the effective projection of your own unique personality clearly but simply within the framework of a given type.

To make things easier for you, you should be aware of two things. First you must know yourself, and second, you must know *how you come*

---

*The Academy Players Directory is a listing of actors and actresses represented by agencies.

Juvenile (Stan Kaiser).

22

Leading Man (Russ Alexander).

Character Actor (Bruce Barrington).

Ingénue (Rochelle Kanter).

Leading Lady (Renée Harmon).

Character Actress (Elaine Heim).

across to others. Both of these perceptions must be very clear in your mind before you will be able to project your type effectively as an actor.

HOW TO GET TO KNOW YOURSELF

Getting to know yourself is easier said than done. Society has made us build many layers around our core personality. The unique you can only be discovered by peeling off the layers like those of an onion. A tedious undertaking? Right, so let's have a little patience and fun as we start peeling to get to your own personality and find that "something" that emanates from within and glows around you, that "something" that is your core personality.

First we'll do a little homework. So, relax and put your feet up, sit comfortably, get yourself a tall, cool drink, turn on the music, and enjoy. Now, close your eyes and start dreaming. Imagine that your fairy god-mother floats into the room and is ready to grant you three wishes. She asks you, "If you could be any character you've seen on the screen, stage, TV, or read about in a book, who would you like to be?" If you are a woman, perhaps Scarlett O'Hara immediately comes to mind. You've probably admired her since you were twelve years old after seeing her in *Gone with the Wind*. Scarlett, the vivacious young woman with the sixteen-inch waist, sparkling green eyes, and the determined and captivating personality—this is the person you've always longed to be.

The very next moment you laugh at yourself. Not in a million years could you be Scarlett O'Hara. First, you are a long way removed from the sunny side of twenty, and second, your eyes are brown, and as far as the sixteen-inch waist is concerned, forget it (no one has a sixteen-inch waist anymore). "Fiddlededee," answers your fairy godmother, in true Scarlett fashion, "Granted you cannot cinch your waist down to sixteen inches, but what's wrong with whittling it down a little anyway? You really do need some exercise, my young woman, and your hazel eyes, well, they would be rather nice if you would permit them to sparkle a bit. That certain-something quality that you admire about Scarlett is not so much her looks as it is her determination and vivaciousness. So, what keeps you from being a determined and vivacious you?

By now, the fairy godmother has settled comfortably next to you, she has put up her feet to rest (nowadays, even fairy godmothers have more clients than they can handle). She takes a sip of your tall, cool drink and then grants you your second wish: "Whom do you want to look like?"

"That's easy." You smile. "Naturally I'd like to look like Cheryl Tiegs." You would give anything to look like this cool, sophisticated woman, but what chances do you have? Your hair isn't golden blond, but brown, and recently you had it cut very short, plus you need funds to patronize the haute couture.

"Fiddlededee," answers your fairy godmother again. "What's wrong with letting your hair grow out so that you will achieve the sleek, sophisticated look? And what's wrong with tinting it a few shades lighter? Also, as far as the haute couture is concerned, elegance is not really a matter of having lots of money (although it helps, of course). It's more a matter of knowing about your core personality, your fashion type, figure assets and liabilities, and the knack of adapting current fashion trends. Really using this knowledge and some common sense, you'll look just as sophisticated as Cheryl."

At this point you open your eyes a little, look into the mirror, and lo and behold, you glimpse a determined, golden-blond woman with the proud carriage, small waist, and sparkling eyes that is *you*.

While you admire yourself, the fairy godmother turns to your male friend who has had some time to consider the questions she has already asked you. He has decided that he's the nice, clean-cut "boy next door" type. He answers, "I think I can play anything that comes up in my category."

The fairy godmother shakes her head. "I don't buy that, young man. You are telling me *who* you *think* you are, but not whom you want to be." She goes on explaining that everyone of us throughout life, from kindergarten on, has been conditioned to bow to pressure groups. In some cases such pressure leads to a distorted, unclear perception of oneself, so we come to project the personality we *think* we are but are not. In most cases, however, group pressure leads us to project how we perceive we ought to be.

"Fine," he agrees, "but look at me, I am the perfect juvenile type."

"Right," insists the fairy godmother, "but you are a bland type. There are thousands of you around, and if you want to make it in the business, you had better try to be more unique."

"Well," he laughs, embarrassed, "I always admired the Three Musketeers, you know, the Dumas classic. Those guys were so flamboyant, so dashing, and they always won, no matter what. Also, I really admire Robert Redford. He has something so confident about him, yet he's warm and friendly. But c'mon, I could never model myself on those guys, I'm still a kid. I just turned eighteen, and I've always been a little shy. Besides, I'm dark-complected. I couldn't be like Redford in a million years."

"Give me a break," sighs the fairy godmother before she admonishes him. "Of course, no actor should try to become a carbon copy of a star he admires. What sells is *uniqueness*." She goes on, "What you admire most in those characters is their exciting qualities. The Musketeers' flamboyance is inherent in your own personality. Because it is true that we admire in others what we really possess way down inside ourselves but which we haven't permitted to surface because such qualities might be in opposition to the personality that others have stamped upon us. Don't mind that you are younger than the characters that you admire or that you don't look like Robert Redford. Take a grain of the Musketeers' dash, add a teaspoon of Robert Redford's warmth, pour in an ounce of his confidence, and presto, you will have a much more effective personality. You will be unique, because all of these qualities *are* part of your own core personality. Just permit all of these qualities to come forth, let them shine. Yes, you'll still look the same, you'll still be a juvenile, but you won't be bland anymore or like a thousand others your age. You will be special and you will be *you*."

Your fairy godmother now takes a quick look at her watch before she grants the third wish: "You will both project your personalities effectively." But remember, what good does it do if you see yourselves as vivacious, determined, dashing, and warm but you do not project this to others? You may be coming across to others as too dull or too aggressive. If you are too dull, you'll blend in with the wall and miss out on a good many opportunities in life. Someone else will walk away with the parts you wanted, and people will take you for granted and leave you alone. You will not come across in interviews or shine in cold readings no matter how sensitive and creative you are. Many actors with bland personalities literally hide behind the characters they portray. These actors may achieve some success on the stage, but will encounter greater difficulty with film and television as both media demand strong projections of one's own personality.

So, what should you do? Well, just become a little more assertive in your dress and behavior, more outgoing, make other people notice you. (Join an improvisational class; this would be ideal for you.)

Now, what if you're too aggressive? Ask four to six friends how they feel about your behavior. Maybe this is just the opportunity they've been waiting for to tell you about your desire to outshine everyone else, your habit of always having the last word. Well, at least you assert yourself and people notice you, but you must discover the root of this unpleasant behavior pattern. This kind of display is most probably a sign of insecurity. Many deeply frustrated actors present a blustering, pushy facade. They have a "chip on their shoulder" to compensate for feelings of inferiority. Usually such feelings have their roots in the fact that these actors are uncertain in their craft or unhappy about their looks. If you fall into this category, you would do well to change what is amiss. Get more training, go to a new coach, join the workshop that you've wanted to join for a long time but were afraid you might not do well in. If it's your looks, then change what you can, go on a diet, build up those flabby muscles, get your nose fixed if it bothers you, go to a dermatologist and clear up your skin. Try graciously to accept what you cannot change, but the things you can, please change quickly.

Often it is your behavior and not your looks or acting ability that will keep you from giving a good reading or getting the part. Your negative feelings transmit themselves to others no matter how friendly you act.

If each and every person you meet forms a different opinion of you, be aware that this is a clue that you do not project a *definite* personality of your own, but rather change like a chameleon, reflecting the personality of the person with you at the moment. If this happens to you, do all you can to get in touch with yourself and find the hidden personality that you are most comfortable with for yourself, not others. This chameleon-personality projection will cripple if not destroy the confidence you must have if you are to survive in the film business. You must accept the fact that you are a person of merit and worth and are not dependent on others for approval. We all have to face the pressures of conformity, we all have to adjust to it, yet we must take care not to let it destroy our uniqueness.

Try to achieve a balance between the personal *you* and what is expected of this *you*. If you find yourself uncomfortable with the demands of your surrounding environment, then it might be time to change your environment. It may not be you who chafes against people or circumstances, but you may live in an environment for which you are unsuited. Therefore, as you search for this *unique you*, always remember that it is you who must be *comfortable* with your personality projection, not your coach, your aunt, or your boyfriend.

CREATE A CLEAR FASHION IMAGE FOR YOURSELF

Once you've gotten to know yourself, once you've created the type that you can project and feel comfortable with, you have to take another step. You have to dress to *enhance* your type and make that type *immediately recognizable*. Yes, people do judge a book by its cover. If someone gave you an expensively wrapped present, you wouldn't expect to find cheap paper clips inside. On the other hand, if you were given a plain paper bag, you also wouldn't expect to find a gold necklace inside. This holds true for people as well. *Your first impression is a lasting one.* So, you'd better make it a favorable one.

Have you ever wondered why you feel so much better in one outfit than in another? It's because the one you feel so good in is *right for your type.* We can safely say that the wise actor chooses clothes that are the reflections of his own unique personality. In a sense he uses the visual elements of garments and accessories to create a product of self-expression, the picture of the personality he presents to the world.

Let's take a closer look at the style identities. We'll discuss the women's first. Whether you are a leading lady or a character actress, you will fall within one of the following fashion categories.

The Classic

The first of the four basics is the classic. This type of woman chooses structured, tailored lines. She prefers solid colors in silks, cotton, and linen. Quality is her need, not quantity. She chooses genuine jewelry, putting her money in one good piece rather than buying several pieces of inferior quality. Her handbag is simple and made of real leather. Her dresses are unadorned and the fine fabric speaks for itself. She prefers classic pumps and limits the use of her print scarves. The classic velvet blazer is her trademark.

The classic is a great style for the woman over thirty-five. For the younger woman, this style is less desirable, not because of the outlay of money involved, but because this style is too structured and severe to compliment her appearance.

If, in terms of age, figure, and personality, you are right for the classic, you've made a wise decision. Not only will you always look elegant, but you can wear these garments for years. The classic is the style of the super-rich women you see on Park Avenue in New York, in the Cafe Florian in Venice, or in the lobby of the George V in Paris and the Vier Jahreszeiten in Munich.

True, your first investment will be heavy, but because this style is a lasting one, your dollar value per wearing is high. You will be able to buy expensive items on sale, and since the classic never goes out of fashion, the silk blouse you buy on sale this summer, will be good for many summers to come.

Still, there are some inherent dangers in the classic. Because it is a simple, sophisticated style, you should be extra careful not to look dowdy. First of all, pay close attention to the perfect fit of each garment, and second, make your outfits interesting by outstanding color combinations and the clever use of accessories.

Also, if you are under five feet four inches and a little ample or rounded, you should stay away from the classic. If you enjoy the simple line of the classic but are not quite right for it, then turn your eyes to the country casual.

The Country Casual

Here comes the country casual, the second of the basic four. She chooses separates whenever possible—sweaters, tops, blouses, skirts, and slacks. Nubby, strong textures are her favorites. She adores wool capes, lives in boots, loafers, and espadrilles. Fun costume jewelry is her choice, and in its creativity perfectly right for her. She chooses prints, including small checks and narrow stripes. Country casual is a truly young, free, but sensible style. A very marvelous style type. As with the classic, the country casual is a style that one can wear for years to come and discover fantastic buys during sales. You may have to wait for those sales, as country casual is not all that inexpensive.

The disadvantage in the country casual look is not in the style itself but in the fact that it is such a comfortable style that many women get drawn to it for this reason alone and are more interested in the comfort than in the look of their garments.

The country casual woman should make her outfits eye-catching by selecting interesting combinations of texture as well as of pattern and by choosing bright accessories and colors. Many women who are drawn to this style do not feel comfortable in dresses, claiming that they are too frilly or too boring. Still, there are many simple and youthful dresses on the market that are just right for the country casual woman.

The Romantic

Three cheers for number three, the romantic. The soft and feminine looks in both material and lines are her desire. This is a style truly flattering to women from eighteen to eighty. The emphasis on this style is always *softness*. The romantic prefers draped designs and selects delicate floral prints. She enjoys the smooth texture of voile, jersey, sheer cottons, and velvet. She prefers high-heeled sandals over the classic pumps and even gets away with wearing them with slacks. Her jewelry consists of pearls, antique items, and fine gold. The tailored skirt is not for her; she chooses the softer wraparound. Whenever she can, she tops her jeans and slacks with a flowery ruffled blouse.

The romantic is probably the most feminine of all fashion styles and definitely the most flattering for *all* figure types. But, as in every style, the romantic, too, has some dangers.

Since the romantic is so firmly established in our minds as a look of the very young, we tend to forget that it can easily be adapted to all ages, and therefore, women over thirty are often reluctant to give it a try. The key word in the style of the romantic is *adaptable*. Also remember, the basis of the romantic is softness, in both fabric and design. Depending on your age, you might avoid the obvious trappings of the style, such as a lot of lace, flounces, and ribbons. It also goes without saying that for a business meeting you should not float into the boardroom wearing your most flowery dress.

The Ingénue

If you are the ingénue stylewise, then you are very young, between fourteen and twenty-one. You are the woman who looks simply grand in jeans and tops, attire that has become (especially here in Hollywood) somewhat of a uniform for you. It is convenient, good-looking, but a little boring, don't you agree? For this reason we'll break down the ingénue into the following variations.

THE CALIFORNIA GIRL. If you are the outdoors, athletic type, the woman who lives in jeans and tops, you are the California girl. (It also helps if you are tall, blond, and blue-eyed.) You could very well adapt to the look of the country casual, since you do not so much choose the standards of this style as all the fun elements, such as the unusual tops, the great-looking slacks, the jackets, and the creative jewelry. Use all of these elements, but go all out, make everything young, young, young and exciting. Wear your T-shirts and jeans, but make them eye-catching by the clever use of fun jewelry, an extraordinary bag, a scarf you wind around your waist, and so on. Let your fashion creativity go sky-high.

THE STUDIOUS GIRL. Another subtype of the ingénue is the studious girl. (She will probably move later on toward the classic.) Many women in this category, especially if they have started their first job, make the mistake of wearing definitely classic outfits. These garments make them appear too severe, too old, and, well, let's be frank, boring. The classic style is wrong for the studious girl. She, too, should look toward the country casual for some guidelines. Instead of the classic suit, she should wear a skirt and blazer. Instead of the shirtwaist, she should wear a young-looking knit dress. The studious girl will stay away from fun jewelry, such as shell necklaces and wooden pendants (which look so great on the California girl), and wear simple silver and gold items. Everything a little more on the conservative side is right for her. She dresses quietly, but with a little dash, emphasizing her lovely face and figure.

THE YOUNG ROMANTIC. This type has been especially created for you, the soft, feminine woman. You are the one who looks breathtaking in all those laces and ruffles. A word of advice is needed, don't overdo it because *simplicity* is the key word for the young romantic. When you wear that pretty flowery dress, do not divide the attention by adding a ribbon somewhere. Do not overdo a good thing by wearing sparkling jewelry; soft pearls or a delicate gold chain is best fashionwise.

Men have it a little easier than women because their fashion categories are less diversified.

The Juvenile

No matter what your type—California beach boy, clean-cut boy next door, studious young man, or street type—jeans and a T-shirt, sport shirt, or sweater are almost a uniform for you. It goes without saying that the jeans and the T-shirt must be super clean; a soiled T-shirt is definitely not the mark of a good actor. If you are reading for a street type, you can add a leather jacket or cap to give identity to your character.

The Executive Type

You cannot go wrong by adapting the style of a successful businessman. This doesn't mean that you will have to spend a great deal of money on your clothes, since how you wear your clothes is as important as what you wear. You should dress in a quiet, dignified manner. Your best bets are suits. The colors that will most enhance the executive look are dark blue and dark gray suits. Solids are the best choice, but if you prefer a pattern, choose a muted one. You would also do well to stay away from contrasting stitching and piping. The single-breasted suit is your best choice, since it will stay in style for many years to come.

The important fact about your suits is that they fit well. Nothing destroys the projection of the executive look more than an ill-fitting suit. Never wear short-sleeve shirts under your suit jacket. An inch of cuff should show at the sleeve. White shirts are the best choice to go with dark suits. Colored shirts will not convey the crisp impression you want to give for this type. The collar of your shirt should look natural and in no way constrict your neck movements.

You should avoid heavy-soled shoes and stay with the Gucci type of loafer footwear. No matter how hot the day may be, your choice of socks should be the executive full-length style, since short socks always appear rumpled, and if your trousers should ride up, you want a smooth leg line.

Use restraint in your ties. Subdued stripes, small polka dots, and paisley patterns are always attractive and do not draw attention away from your face. Stay away from all sprawling designs, and, if possible, choose your tie in a color that is monochromatic with that of your suit.

The jewelry you select to wear should be absolutely plain. Don't wear showy cuff links and tie clasps. If you wear a tie clasp, it should be worn low enough so that it won't show when you button your jacket.

If you like to wear a handkerchief in your jacket pocket, use plain white linen and let only a little edge of it show. The handkerchief should be unfolded and natural looking, never folded in a neat triangle.

If you want to appear a little less formal, you might consider a blazer, but avoid all sport shirts and trousers, since these will contradict the look of sophistication you wish to project.

The Outdoor Type

The healthy outdoor look is your biggest asset. In your attire, you should do everything you can to enhance the strength of this look. If you are the Western type, you will look terrific in jeans and Western shirts and at times even may risk wearing Western boots and a cowboy hat, but please don't overdo it. Don't wear shiny belt buckles that will tempt any cattle rustlers to target practice. Don't detract from your good looks by wearing heavy silver jewelry around your neck and wrists. In short, use restraint in the Western look.

Sport shirts and trousers are always attractive. You can't go wrong in such an outfit. Make sure your clothes fit properly, and avoid suits, because they are too formal for you. If you want to wear a jacket, choose a suede or smooth leather, since these will enhance your rugged looks.

The Intellectual Type

The intellectual type should strive for a relaxed, comfortable look. Neither suits nor sport shirt and trousers will do, because suits are too stringent for you and restrict your personality too much. Sport shirts and trousers, no matter how subdued, will overpower you. Your best choices are trousers and turtleneck sweaters. If a sweater is not exactly flattering to your build because you are on the heavy side, then a shirt and a loosely hanging cardigan will do quite well. If you wish to dress a little more formally, then choose the blazer look. Blazers should be in dark blue and gray, single-breasted, worn with dark trousers and a white long-sleeve shirt. You might also like a sport jacket in a lightweight tweed. The tweed should be subdued and small in its pattern. I would advise against ties, since they are too restricting and formal in appearance. Here again, the lightweight Gucci loafer is fitting for the style, and as far as socks are concerned, you will feel more comfortable in the snug-fitting full-length type. The intellectual should stay away from jewelry.

Each of you—the executive type, the outdoor type, and the intellectual type—should pay attention to the following details in your outfits:

- The collar of your jacket should be high enough to cover the back of your neck
- The trouser length should break over your shoes.
- Trousers should not be baggy.
- Jackets, even though well fitted, should never be snug, but rather hang relaxed.

THE USE OF COLOR
IN MEN'S FASHIONS

Since men's fashions are simpler in design than women's, color is what gives emphasis to your look. The study of color, as far as psychological impact is concerned, is a relatively new field. Many new discoveries have been made. At this point I will not discuss how the use of color affects the wearer, but rather how it affects the observer and his or her response to you. Consider color as you buy or dress for that important interview. The predominant male colors are

- Black
- Brown
- Gray
- Dark Blue

BLACK. Black denotes power of the highest rank. It is a threatening color, which immediately creates emotional distances. If you are up for "the Villain" part, be he the executive or the outdoor type, black will enhance your devious ways. If you are interviewing for a street-gang type, a black leather jacket will do the trick.

BROWN. Brown is the color of friendliness and compassion. It also denotes a moderate degree of power and strength. If you are the intellectual type, all shades of brown will benefit your personality projection effectively.

GRAY. Gray is a cold color. The color of stone and iron. Gray denotes strength, and it definitely conveys that "I mean business" attitude. Gray is the color chosen by executives.

DARK BLUE. Dark blue also denotes strength and power. It is a very effective color, since it displays these attributes without the "coldness" that gray conveys. It is the color mostly preferred by businessmen and is also excellent for the executive.

THE TOTAL LOOK

Once you have chosen the fashion image that best suits your personality, you should strive for a total look. The clothes you choose should not only enhance you and your personality, they should also interpret instantly the *type* you present. Immediately you should be recognizable as the young housewife next door, the executive, the intellectual, the California girl, the romantic, and so on.

This total look must encompass everything, even your hair style. It goes without saying that the executive should not sport long hair that hangs below his collar. The outdoor and the intellectual types can wear the tousled look well. The romantic should not wear the severe look of the classic, and the classic in turn does not look well with her hair pulled back or loosely hanging, although this look is great for the country casual.

Once you have discovered the *unique you,* you must strive to project your personality, not only in demeanor but also in your dress and hairstyle.

YOUR
PICTURES

3

HOW TO SELECT
A PHOTOGRAPHER

Photographs are the actor's most important tool. They serve as his or her calling card and personal trademark. You will introduce yourself to agents and casting directors through your pictures. Therefore, it stands to reason that when you walk into an office, your pictures should resemble you as closely as possible.

Agents and casting directors are generally seeking an attractive look, something *captivating,* though not necessarily beautiful. Something that will make a person look at a face and think, "Well, that's the kind of person I would like to see." Most likely this elusive, captivating "something" is expressed in your eyes and mouth. You should strive for clean, dynamic photographs, well-lit faces, in short, pictures that are *natural, alive,* and have *energy.*

Therefore, choosing the right photographer is an important decision. First, we'll discuss the kind of photographers you should not choose. Tops on the list is your Uncle Jamie, who always takes such marvelous wedding and birthday pictures. True, he may be a terrific photographer, but he sees you as his niece or nephew, *not* as the actor you are. So please forget about Uncle Jamie.

You may look at the photos displayed in your favorite department store, and since you have a charge account there, it might seem like a good idea to let them take your pictures. Wrong again. It's true that the people who work in the department store studio are well trained and often artists in their field, but they are trained to take *family* pictures, not pictures for actors' and actresses' portfolios. The pictures they take will be attractive and well lit, but you run the risk of them not being as dynamic as you might desire them to be.

So, forget about the department store and consider the models' photographer. You have seen her or his pictures in magazines, and they are wow. Maybe this photographer is a little expensive, but you're willing to borrow some money for your career. Hold your horses, don't run to the first bank. This person, no matter how excellent, is not for you, the *actor*. Think about it, he or she takes pictures of models, right? Fashion models modeling clothing, posing. An actor's pictures should be completely *natural*. Posing yourself, no matter how glamorous, would be detrimental, because it displays you as a model, not the actor that the agent and casting director are seeking.

If you live in Los Angeles or New York, your best bet is to find someone either by word of mouth, through the Yellow Pages, or among the photographers who advertise in the trades.*

You may live in a small town and have access only to the local photographer, but if you follow some simple rules, you will have some professional pictures to show for your effort:

- Flip through some magazines and select some pictures that display energy and vitality but at the same time are neither posed or phony. Take these pictures to your photographer.
- Practice this look of vitality in front of your mirror.
- Follow the suggestions about actor's photography that you find on the next few pages.
- Don't let photographers talk you into "glamour shots" or let them take a "yearbook picture."

The photographers advertising in the trades are usually dependable and reasonable. These photographers are trained to take actors' pictures. It is their job, and they make a good living at their profession. Their fees vary a great deal, but you might get twelve headshots for between $50 and $100.

The first step in selecting one of these photographers is to call and find out their fee. If the price is right, make an appointment to view their pictures. See if their style of photography is to your liking, then find out if you feel comfortable with the photographer, whether you can talk to him or

Trades is the industry term for newspapers and magazines that report only film, TV, cable, and theatrical news.

her easily and, most important, find out if the photographer sees you as you see yourself. This is a prime factor, for you must be able to communicate to that person *what you want* and *how you want to come across.* Don't leave this up to the photographer. Don't let him lead you toward a type that doesn't suit you. Know your own type and stick to it.

PUTTING YOUR BEST FOOT FORWARD

Once you have decided on the photographer, make an appointment for your best time of day, the time when you feel especially bright-eyed, bushy-tailed, and full of energy.

You should take with you at least two well-fitting tops in addition to what you will be wearing. It is best to choose unadorned garments so as not to detract from your face. Your hair should be just right, somewhere in-between haircuts. Some photographers suggest the services of a makeup artist, whose fee ranges from twenty-five to fifty dollars. For the young woman under twenty-five, I feel this is a waste of money, because the makeup artist may take your good natural, individual appearance and turn you into some boring glamorous type. For the woman over thirty, however, the makeup artist is a must and can bring out your best features. Don't try to save a few dollars by applying your own makeup, no matter how skilled you may be, since the makeup artist uses special techniques for black and white photography that are very different from everyday makeup. Don't be dismayed after being made up if you look into the mirror and see a face that resembles a clown from outer space—the black and white picture will come out terrific.

YOUR HEADSHOT

The first and most important picture is your headshot. The headshot is a must for the beginning actor. A new headshot is also important if you have been using one for several months without any results or if you've changed your hair color or style. A headshot is an 8-by-10-inch glossy photo, generally shot indoors, where the photographer can control the lighting. Some photographers prefer outdoor headshots, others moody artistic lighting, but both will do you a disservice, because you need well-lit photos, which can only be achieved under controlled conditions in a studio.

You should know some salient facts concerning this all-important headshot, your trademark and calling card. First, don't perform a role within the headshot. For example, don't wear a police officer's cap or a doctor's white coat and stethoscope. Don't wave a soft drink can or beer can. These kinds of pictures are fine for your portfolio but will be detrimental for the headshot. Remember, the headshot is you, not some character you are portraying. Second, don't distract the viewer by dressing too busily. A small print or a solid color will do fine. I'll admit that this sounds rather drab, but don't even try to perk up this plain look with a scarf or some jewelry. Remember, you want to shine, not the outfit you're wearing. Use no hats, because there is nothing more distracting in a headshot than a hat. As far as color is concerned, avoid wearing either black or white, since neither photographs well. For men, blazers, plaid sport shirts, and sweaters are the best choice. If you are a woman, avoid plunging necklines.

Don't have your pet dog or cat in the photo with you; your pet might get the part instead of you. Avoid any kind of busy background— another reason why headshots should be taken in a studio rather than outdoors.

Don't have your pictures touched up. You should look exactly like your pictures. If you are a character actress, you will want each little laugh line and charming wrinkle to be clearly visible. You'll be happily surprised how valuable these little lines can be, for they may bring you the role you've always coveted.

Well, the don'ts have been rather lengthy, now we'll talk about the do's.

Do look yourself. Get a picture that says, "Hi, this is me." Look energetic and full of life. This doesn't necessarily mean you have to smile, since a serious picture can convey as much energy as a smiling one. Look right into the camera. This is very important. In your headshot you should look neither up nor down. If you are looking right at the camera, it gives you that important energetic look. Be sure to project that captivating vitality in your eyes and mouth.

So, now you have had your important headshot taken. You sigh with relief and wait a few days for your proofs. Your heart is pounding and your hands shake a little as you inspect the proof sheet. You look at yourself, this strange, exciting person who is on her or his way to becoming a film actor.

The first look at a proof sheet can be very confusing, so don't select your headshot right this minute. Take your time and give your emotions a chance to settle down. It's a good idea to let your photographer pick the first choice. With lightning speed he will run down the columns of the proof sheet, simulating the way an agent or casting director will look at the photos. Let the photographer circle the pictures that immediately grab his or her attention. *Immediacy* is the key factor in selecting a headshot. You need a picture that immediately demands attention, since agents and casting directors do not look at every photo carefully, but select only those that reach out to them quickly, those that stand out in some way or other.

Take the proofs home and pore over them. Get some outside opinions, as it is very difficult to be objective. You may select a flattering picture that looks great but not really like you or one that is lacking immediacy. Ask your friends and relatives what they think, but don't rely too heavily on their advice. They tend to see you as they know you rather than as the actor you are. The best advice can be given by your agent if you have one already. Your agent picked you because she or he sees a certain quality in you and wants your pictures to reflect that quality.

Once you have narrowed your choice down to, say, three or four, take a magnifying glass and examine the pictures for any apparent flaws, such as circles under your eyes or too much gum showing in your smile. Look for tension around your mouth and any unflattering shadows. After the final selection has been made, ask your photographer to make an 8-by-10-inch *glossy* of the picture. Do not accept a matte finish, because it will not reproduce properly. Take your glossy to a photo lab that specializes in quality photos and have a negative made of your picture, which you will keep. Have your name put on your picture negative and then order between 50 and 100 glossies.

You should refrain at this time from having any composite pictures taken. You will not need composites at the time of your headshot. The reason for this is that various agents may see you as different types, and the agent who signs you will want to decide what kind of commercial composite shots you should have taken. With this knowledge and the blessing of your agent, you will end up with a much better composite.

YOUR COMPOSITES

Composites are 8-by-10-inch printed pictures that have your headshot trademark with your name on the front plus four smaller pictures in various outfits and situations on the back. There are three kinds of composites: theatrical composites, commercial composites, and modeling composites.

Theatrical Composites

Theatrical composites are not so popular as they were a few years ago. But if you are a leading lady or leading man, such composites are still in vogue, since they will be submitted for roles in which you and your personality are of prime importance.

If you fall into this category, avoid showing pictures that portray different moods and attitudes when you select the four small pictures for the back of your composite. Don't try to impress by showing different types of characters that you can portray. These kinds of pictures are completely wrong for a theatrical composite. All that is required are shots of your face, so that the casting director can determine how well you photograph from all angles.

On the front of the composite will be your trademark picture. If this is a smiling one, you should have a serious picture on the back of your composite and vice versa. Also it is important to have a profile shot. If you are blessed with a good profile—and you'll be amazed how few actors are—you could cash in on that point. On the other hand, if your nose is too short, too long, maybe not quite straight, or your chin recedes, you might prefer a three-quarter shot instead of a full profile, since that angle would be the more flattering.

You will also need a full shot. A full shot is a photo that displays your entire figure. Don't choose a bikini shot if you are a woman or bathing shorts if you are a man, unless your figure is a whooping 10. Any picture showing you from head to toe, simply and comfortably dressed, will serve the purpose. For women I would suggest a skirt instead of jeans or slacks, so that a casting director can rest assured that your legs are nothing to be ashamed of and you can easily be filmed walking down a hallway.

The fourth picture should show you in a sports activity. This doesn't mean a posed picture, but rather an action shot that will convey energy and health, both so beloved by agents and casting directors.

If you want to have some character shots for your agent and to carry in your portfolio, this is fine. Here different hats, hairdos, and costumes are great. Carefully chosen props might perk up this kind of shot. You can show yourself as the powerful executive in one shot and the kindly doctor in another. The ingenue might have a picture that shows her as the girl next door and another that shows her as the studious college student. *Remember not to change your personality too drastically. Remain the same person, looking just a little different each time.*

The actor who has primarily been stage-trained or the actor coming with his B.F.A. in Drama straight from college or any actor who has been trained to portray characters might view this approach as almost sacriligious, but this is the way it is in the film business. The fact that you can portray both Laurie in *Oklahoma* and one of the old maids in *Arsenic and Old Lace* will not matter here at all. SAG has a very large membership of actors and doesn't need you to play an older person, since they can find easily anyone they want.

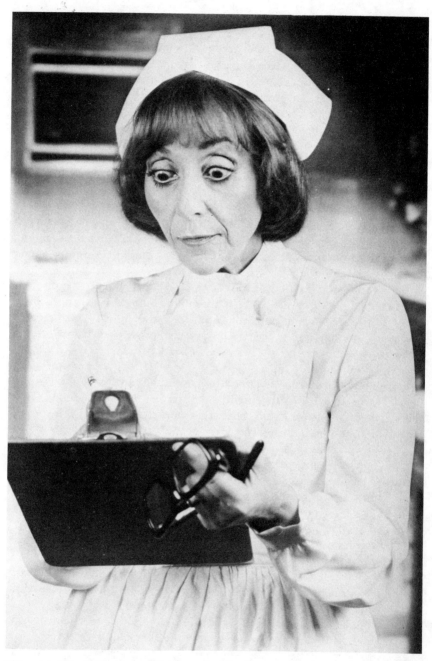

This and the following photos are excellent examples of pictures for commercial composites. Distraught nurse (Arlene Gould).

Friendly waitress (Molly Golaner).

Efficient Painter (June Mellon).

Commercial Composites

Commercial composites are as different from theatrical composites as a county fair is from an afternoon tea party. Don't think you can use one for the other. On the front of your commercial composite, your headshot trademark will be featured the same way it is on your theatrical composite. Don't choose a different headshot, since you will want to acquaint commercial and theatrical agents as well as casting directors with your face and name. The difference between these two kinds of composites are *type, energy,* and *immediacy.*

First we will take a look at type. Please remember that you have only thirty seconds in a commercial to bring forth the demanded message. Truly a frighteningly short time to establish your personality and sell a product as well. The audience has to recognize immediately the character who either enjoys a hamburger, drives a Rolls-Royce, or uses this particular brand of dog food or detergent. There has to be a symbiotic relationship between the actor and the product advertised. In your picture you can achieve this immediacy by putting yourself in a situation that your character type might find himself in and by reacting to it in an unusual and interesting way. Avoid using cliché expressions, and really try to understand how the character would feel in a given situation. Look at the pictures. Study the distraught nurse, the friendly waitress, the efficient painter. You will notice that the actress on film is always the same type, the best type suited for the circumstances.

A high energy level is a must on your commercial composite. Only a person of high energy grabs a viewer's attention in the first two seconds of a commercial. Your pictures must convey this ability. Don't confuse high energy with "pushing" emotions, that is to say, high voice volume and broad gestures. High energy is inherent in the actor's vitality. Even "soft" commercials, such as those selling perfume and makeup, demand a certain vitality radiating from the performer.

Modeling Composites

Modeling composites are the third type of composites we are dealing with here and are only used if you go out for *printwork.* If you intend to specialize in fashion photography, which is the most important area of printwork, you'd do well to tackle this difficult field *only* if you are over 5 feet 6 inches, very thin, and have had some modeling training.

The pictures on your modeling composite should show your ability to model clothes, and therefore you would do well to use the classical model poses you were taught in school.

These pictures should not be taken by the same photographer who took your commercial or theatrical pictures. You need a photographer who specializes in fashion photography.

YOUR PORTFOLIO

A portfolio is the attaché-case leather bag that actors guard so jealously while waiting to be called in for their interviews. If you are just starting out, casting directors will spend little if no time looking at your portfolio, because they know they will see the same pictures that are on your composite, except in an 11-by-14-inch format. So, if you can somehow persuade the casting director to glance at your portfolio, now is the time to show her or him your *other looks,* the *different characters* you are able to portray within the framework of your own personality. Your portfolio should realistically show the roles you can play. A word of warning here: If you are an actress/model or actor/model, do not lace your actor's portfolio with pictures that were taken at a modeling session. They will be too posed and will consequently be a drawback to your being hired as an actor.

Later on, when you have gained experience, the portfolio will be an important tool for you. You will carry production stills, pressbooks, ad slicks, along with newspaper ads and reviews of the films, stage productions, and such in which you have appeared.

YOUR RESUME

For many agents and casting directors, the résumé is even more important than the picture for determining whether to call you in for an interview, to file your picture for further consideration, or to throw it in the wastebasket.

Your résumé should be *short*. Absolutely no more than one mimeographed page. The basic function of the résumé is to inform your prospective employer of your experience as an actor. Your hobbies, hopes and aspirations, likes and dislikes, have no place in your résumé. The résumé itself should be *neat*. Remember, the résumé reflects more about your personality than a picture. If words are misspelled, the typing is sloppy, the photocopying carelessly done, or, even worse, if the résumé arrives with traces of your lunch, including coffee strains or grease spots, then it shows that you are not proud of your accomplishments or of yourself. You may be a terrific-looking, highly talented, and sensitive actor, but if you are careless as far as your résumé is concerned, then it stands to reason that you may be as careless in your work.

Be sure to staple your résumé to your picture securely. Do not use a paper clip or tape. There is nothing more annoying than wanting to call an actor in for a reading, only to find there is no name on the picture and the résumé that was attached via a paper clip has now vanished into thin air, never to be seen again.

Your résumé should be arranged in such a way that a casting director can find out at a glance about your credits and your background.

Résumés come in two categories: *professional*, which includes

LIZA MITCHELL
SAG

Actors Agency   Height: 5'7"
39 Sunset Lane   Weight: 120 lbs.
Hollywood CA 90046   Eyes: Brown
Tel: 213–467–1342   Hair: Brown

FILM

High School Capers--Featured--Independent Films, World-Wide
                                Films Release, 1982
Monster Attack   --Featured--Coronado Company, ACE Asso-
                                ciates (overseas) 1981
My Mother and Me --Star   --USC Cinema Dept., Los Angeles
                                Grad Thesis, 1982

TELEVISION

"Hart to Hart"   --Bit   --"No Escape"--Spelling Goldberg
                                Productions, 1980

STAGE

Mary Mary   --Mary   --Valley Community Theater,
                                Reseda, 1982
Forty Karats   --Tina   --Dinner Theater, Pasadena, 1982

COMMERCIALS

List upon request

TRAINING

B.A. in Drama, UCLA, 1980
"On Camera"--Film Acting Workshop
Lou Bakers's Commercial Workshop
Stella Stearn--Drama School

WORKSHOPS

The Improvisational Group, Hollywood
Comedy Workshop (presently in attendance)

SPECIAL ABILITIES

Ballet (pro)   Voice (mezzo)

SPORTS

Tennis   Swimming   Horseback riding

FOREIGN LANGUAGE

French (fluent)

legitimate stage and screen credits, and *beginner's,* for those actors who have not yet earned such credits.

Let's take a look at the professional résumé first. On the following page you will find a sample of an acceptable professional résumé. (The names of acting schools, films, and production firms are fictional, of course.)

THE PROFESSIONAL RESUME

Liza's résumé states her name and union affiliations at the top of the page. At the left-hand corner she has listed her agent's name, address, and telephone number. It is best to omit your own telephone number, since your agent will handle all upcoming negotiations. However, you should list your answering service. Liza lists all of her vital statistics, such as height, weight, color of hair and eyes. These statistics are important, since they will save time for the casting director and agent who are looking for a diminutive woman to play opposite a short actor. Liza is a tall 5 feet 7 inches. You will notice she did not put her age on the résumé, nor does she list an age range. If you are a child or teenager, then you must include your age, but once you have arrived at the ripe old age of twenty, it is better to avoid all reference to age. If Liza were to decide, for any reason, to list her age, she would list an age range from eighteen to twenty-eight, which tells the casting director that her real age is about twenty-three. A good rule to follow is to count down five years and count up five years. Still, by giving an age range, you may maneuver yourself into a corner. If your chronological age is twenty-five but you look much younger and could be right for the role of an eighteen-year-old, by looking at your age range, the casting director may disqualify you for this particular role. In commercials you will not be able to play younger than you really are anyway, and it is best to let the casting people decide how old or young you can look.

The first item on Liza's list on the résumé is *film.* If she were living in New York, she would list her *stage credits* first, because stage credits take precedence in New York, whereas film credits take precedence in Los Angeles. She lists her *last* film role first. It is to her benefit that this role was recent, because it shows her to be *current.* This is a strong point to be considered by the casting director. She also shows the years the films were shot, listing first the *name of the film,* next the category of her part. Liza was *featured,* which means she had a nice little role in the film. Next she lists *the production company* and the name of the *distribution company.* The latter is of prime importance to the casting people. Unless the film was produced by a major studio or a big independent, chances are the film may never see the screen. By knowing the name of the distribution company, the casting people will know that the film will be shown domestically.* If the film has no domestic distribution as of yet but is being shown overseas, this should be noted next to the name of the distribution company (as in the case of Liza's second entry). She also lists a student film that was done at a well-known college. She does well to list this film.

The second item on Liza's résumé is *Television.* She lists *the name of the television show, the segment in which she appeared, the size of her role,* and *the distribution company.*

Then Liza lists her *stage* experience. As you can see, even though her work has not been earth-shattering, she does have some experience as far as stage is concerned. She lists the name of the play, the character she portrayed, and the place where she performed. In this case, she performed at a dinner theater (non-union) and a community theater. Liza wisely included these meager credits on her résumé. The stage experience will serve her well if she applies for a film or television show cast out of New York or if the casting director in Hollywood has been based in New York. Many casting directors who are working or have previously worked in New York feel strongly that the Hollywood actor lacks important stage experience and is therefore "too laid back" for many roles. In Hollywood, their counterparts swear that the stage-trained actor projects too much, is often artificial, and lacks the personality of the screen-trained actor. As in most cases, both sides have their points; but honestly, stage experience is an important phase in an actor's development. Since you do not know whether the casting director for whom you will be reading subscribes to the New York or the Hollywood creed, you should make sure that your stage and film credits are fairly balanced. This way everyone is happy.

Under the heading Television Liza lists *commercials.* She states that she will submit a "list upon request." If she were to list her commercial credits, she would do so in this order: First the *name of the product,* then the *name of the production company,* last her category: principal. This tells us that she either had lines (a speaking part) or was featured principally on the screen. If Liza has a long list of commercial credits, then it might be to her advantage not to list them, since the casting director could decide against her, considering her to be *overexposed.* On the other hand, if she listed only one credit for a commercial, the casting director might decide against her because of *lack of experience.* So the term "list upon request" will serve you best.

Training is the next item to be listed. This might be omitted as soon as you have accumulated a substantial list of credits. But even when

---

Domestically shown means within the limits of the United States.

you acquire such credits, it is still wise to list the names of notable coaches who have given you training, such as Lee Strasberg, Uta Hagen, or Stella Adler. This shows that you have talent, since these coaches accept only talented actors in their classes.

In the beginning of every actor's career, the information given under the heading *Training* will be almost as important as any TV or film credits. Most casting directors are familiar with the better known acting teachers, what kind of training and techniques they use, and what kind of acting they stress, so even if you are not a student of one of the world-renowned teachers, if you come from a well-established and recognized acting school, your chances for being called in to read are very good. Most casting directors in Hollywood are uncomfortable if they see no training listed on a résumé. If you are lacking in this area, you should quickly enroll in a reputable film acting school. To work in film and television you should be thoroughly familiar with acting techniques used on the screen and should have a working knowledge of film terminology.

As you can see, Liza has covered both areas sufficiently. She lists a film acting school, a commercial workshop, as well as an acting school. In this way she shows herself to be well prepared for her chosen profession. Her B.A. in Drama adds weight to her experience. It is true that an acting résumé should only give information about an acting background, but a degree in her field shows her to be well read and educated.

Listing her workshops in comedy and improvisation is also important, because many directors feel these techniques especially helpful for the actor who wants to specialize in commercials.

Special abilities are next on her résumé. Her background in this area is not terribly impressive. She dances ballet, and the "pro"* indicates that she is skilled enough in this dance form to survive in a corps de ballet and is definitely no amateur. "Voice (mezzo)" indicates that she has taken some lessons, but since no name of a teacher is given or the term *pro* added, the casting director knows that her voice is probably acceptable but needs training.

Next she lists *sports*. Sports should be listed on every actor's résumé. Every sport that you feel you can do well should be mentioned. It is not necessary that you do any of these sports on a professional level, but you should be skilled enough to perform adequately in front of the camera.

As far as foreign languages and dialects are concerned, Liza mentions only French and adds that she is fluent. It really doesn't pay to list a foreign language unless you can speak it fluently. Also if you have just learned to imitate a British or German accent in your dialect class in college,

*In a résumé, *pro* stands for professional ability.

it will be of little help. Remember, if casting directors want a genuine accent, they have it at the tip of their fingers, since there are 54,000 actor members of SAG.

In conclusion, looking at Liza's résumé, the casting director or agent knows immediately that

- She has prepared herself well for her profession
- While she has no impressive credits, she does have good, solid beginner's credits
- She has worked fairly regularly, and most important, she is *current*
- She is a member of SAG
- Her résumé is neat, brief, and to the point, which shows that she is organized and responsible

No résumé is able to give the scope of your talent, personality, or professionalism, but it can tell the agent and casting director about your abilities and can give them confidence to call you in for an interview.

THE BEGINNER'S RESUME

And now to the type of résumé you must avoid. A great many of this sort "flutter" onto agents' and casting directors' desks, contributing heavily to the consumption of aspirin and other headache-calming medications whenever the poor unsuspecting recipients get a case of the creeps. Are you sitting down? Here we go:

BUNNY BONES   Tel: 369–3446 (don't call me, I'll call you ha ha . . .)

I always wanted to be an actress. Ever since I was a little girl, I've wanted to be a movie star, and I know you can help me. I really have prepared myself to be an actress. I have worked hard, and now I think it's time for me to get an agent. I have played to great acclaim and even signed autographs. I have played the following roles:

Anne	--Midsummer Night's Dream (you guessed it, Shakespeare, good for you)
Anne	--Anne of a Thousand Days (Anderson)
Lucy	--Charlie Brown's Christmas (we wrote that at camp)
Lady Macbeth	--Shakespeare again
Auntie	--Bell, Book, and Candle (I forgot the name of the author)

Hart to Hart   --starring Stephanie Powers (I want to be just like her)
Flowers Must Die--Girl in hospital (My brother was the director in that
                one for his college senior thesis, so he gave me a
                speaking part.)

I have graduated from Valley High School, and I am presently majoring in
Makeup and Hair Styling at a cosmetology school. My hobbies are stamp
collecting, painting, diving, and snow skiing.

Last year I won the downhill skiing championship at Big Bear. I won
summer field competition in skateboarding at my school.

Pretty hopeless, you agree? Right. Bunny's résumé spells *amateur* in capital
letters. No matter how attractive her picture may be, after reaching for the
aspirin bottle, the agent will deposit her résumé in file thirteen, which is
the wastebasket. Mailing in a résumé such as Bunny's leaves her chances of
becoming an actress about as remote as a polar bear in the Antarctic getting
heatstroke.

Let's not give up on Bunny, though. Let's take a look at her chances
after rewriting her résumé.

First of all, she should avoid being funny or cute. A résumé is a
business letter, not a draft for a comedy routine. She would also be wise not
to give out her telephone number, but list her answering service instead. An
answering service only costs a few dollars and will save her from annoying
crank calls.

No one is interested in her desire to become a movie star. She
wouldn't be sending out a résumé if she didn't want to earn her living in the
acting field.

The roles that she lists having played mark her as a rank amateur of
the highest order. Also she doesn't mention the place or theater where she
performed these "roles." This makes it look as though these roles were
probably practice scenes she worked on in her drama class in high school.
This impression is strengthened by the unbelievable range of parts, from an
ingenue (Puck) to a leading lady (Anne) to a character actress (Lady
Macbeth) to a comedy part (Lucy).

Bunny also lists some very impressive television shows, but since
there is no SAG membership listed on her résumé, everyone knows it is
impossible for her to have worked on these shows. This means she worked as
an *atmosphere* or *extra*. Unfortunately such credits do not belong on the
actor's résumé, so besides having no usable stage credits, her impressive
screen credits go down the drain also. Well, not quite. There is an
interesting little item listed. She did have a speaking part in a college thesis
film. Bunny should definitely list this film, cleverly omitting the fact that
her brother directed it.

Yes, college grad and thesis films can go a long way on a beginner's résumé, especially if they are from a school that is well known for its excellent film department.

As I mentioned before, hobbies are of no interest on a résumé and shouldn't be mentioned. Unfortunately she didn't attend any recognizable acting school, nor is she a member of any workshop. Bunny's sports activities are impressive, and she seems to be a whiz in this area. She did win a skiing championship, she is taking diving lessons, and won a prize in skateboarding. She seems to excel in these sports, and for this reason could be of interest to agents and casting directors who are looking for actresses who shine in these areas. Another plus-factor is her skill in makeup and hair styling. These skills may land her a job with a small independent film company as a makeup artist and thereby give her an opportunity to do an "under five-line" acting job in addition to her makeup work.

Rewritten, Bunny's résumé should look like this:

Bunny Bones

Answering Service: 872–3456

Height 5 feet 5 inches
Weight 110 lbs
Hair Blond
Eyes Blue

TRAINING

Member (three years) drama club, Valley High School, Los Angeles

STAGE

"Charlie Brown's Christmas"--Lucy--Valley High School, Los Angeles

FILM

"Flowers Must Die"--featured--UCLA Cinema Dept., Grad Thesis

SPORTS

Skateboarding--First Prize, L.A. High School Competition
Snow Skiing--Winner Championship, Big Bear Mountain
Diving (pro)

SPECIAL ABILITIES

Makeup and Hair Design (pro)

Now Bunny's résumé looks decidedly different. Very honestly it shows that she has no professional training but did participate in a school play and was featured in a college film. She is skilled in makeup and hair design, and, stressing her athletic abilities, she might very well land a commercial agent. Let's assume she doesn't end up with a commercial agent who, after exploiting her athletic abilities, drops her. A reliable agent will positively advise her to get more training and more experience on stage and in films. She would do well at this point in her career to gain experience in college film and community theater productions.

After seeing her first résumé, you might think such naiveté to be farfetched, but this is not so. I have seen many résumés that are similar to hers, and many of these actors have a burning desire to work in their profession. Chances are they might be great or at least acceptable. These actors, too, should have a chance at the "brass ring," but they ruin their chances unknowingly from the beginning since they have no *tools* and no *training*. No carpenter would dream of starting his workday without his tools and would not dare to go looking for a job without the proper training. For some strange reason, many actors feel that they have the right to step on to a stage or in front of a camera without even the slightest knowledge of their craft. Acting is not only talent, energy, vitality, and good looks. It is also the thorough knowledge of how to use your god-given gifts. Acting is not only the joy and release of letting go of your own emotions, it is also the ability to get an audience to participate in your feelings. This takes a lot of training. You also need a basic knowledge of how this business works. One piece of evidence of such knowledge is an acceptable résumé that shows that you know what you're doing.

One last word of advice: Be truthful on your résumé. State only the facts and do not stretch the truth. Agents can be very leery of résumés that have that fictional touch, and this could blow your chances of being seen by them. "How," you ask, "does an agent know if I am telling the truth or not?" Many actors who are completely honest in their personal lives feel they have to "pad" their résumés with a long list of credits. This attitude is wrong. All of you, no matter how few credits are on your résumés, can be proud of what you have done. Don't be afraid to admit that you are just beginning to make a start. We all have to start somewhere. Show that you are continually working on your craft. Be enthusiastic about what you have done and what you are doing. This attitude alone will encourage confidence in the agent and casting director.

HOW TO FIND
AN AGENT

5

The agent is one of the most important people in your acting career. Actors have been made by the right agent and broken by a wrong one. So, the first hurdle actors have to jump in their careers is finding an agent. There are over two hundred agencies in Hollywood alone that are franchised by SAG, but finding an agent is still difficult.

In desperation you might get involved with an agency that you should not really even consider. They are *not* franchised by SAG, and they usually advertise for clients in daily newspapers. However, many reputable SAG-franchised agencies do advertise in *Drama Log* in Hollywood and in *Back Stage* in New York if they are just starting out and in need of new faces. Those agencies you can safely contact. But if you see wording such as, "Looking for new faces, no experience needed, immediate pay," then you should beware, since it probably means there will be immediate pay for the advertiser, but not for you.

Unfortunately, there are a few agencies that prey on the inexperienced or desperate actor. "We have expenses," they convince you as they roll their eyes heavenward. They claim they must pay for mailing out pictures, spend time calling casting offices to make appointments, and for these services they must charge you a "retainer fee." This fee usually ranges from two hundred to five hundred dollars. If you hear these lines, and lines they are, hold on to your checkbook and *run*. You will never get a job or an interview from these "agents."

SAG-franchised agents on the other hand, are not permitted to take any pay until they have gotten you a job. If they get you a non-union job, their fee will be 10 percent of your theatrical, film, or television work. The fee is 15 percent for commercial work and 20 to 25 percent for any printwork done. If the agent negotiates a union, film, or television job, then the producer will pay 10 percent *on top of your pay* to the agent. For a union commercial the fee is 15 percent of your pay. And since printwork is *always* non-union, *you* will pay the required commission. An agent will *never* demand money before *you* have *received* money, please don't forget this.

Other bogus agencies you shouldn't consider are the ones that welcome you with open arms, claiming they have "such terrific vibes about you and know that you are sooooooo talented and in fact that you will be a star in no time at all." Then, while you are still up on cloud nine, they hinge their signing of you upon the requirement that you have your pictures taken by the photographer of their choice and join an acting class that is run by their friend who "lives around the corner."

Remember, the reputable agent will *never* condition your acceptance upon your using the services of a certain acting coach or photographer.

True, if you have only stage experience or are fresh out of college, your agent may stress the need for you to receive some training in the special techniques that are required of a film actor. But only if you ask her will she recommend some well-known and reputable coaches, workshops, or classes in the local community college extension program. She will leave the decision of where to study open to you. The same goes for pictures. Your agent might not like the pictures that you submit to her or may see you quite differently than you see yourself. If you agree she is right as far as your type is concerned and that the pictures don't do you justice, then, *if you ask* her, she will suggest some photographers with whom she is familiar and who have done satisfactory work for her other clients.

Modeling agencies are the only non-SAG-franchised agencies that you can safely deal with. Since these agencies are dealing in printwork, fashion shows, and showroom modeling only, they do not have to be SAG-franchised.

SAG-FRANCHISED AGENCIES

Now that you are familiar with the type of agencies that you should avoid, let's discuss the reputable, franchised agencies. There are about four hundred SAG-franchised agencies in the United States. (Los Angeles, New York, Miami, Denver, Chicago, Las Vegas, San Diego, and Atlanta.) About half of these agencies are located in Hollywood. Hollywood was and still is the center of the movie industry.

These agencies range from such super organizations as the William Morris Agency, which has offices throughout the world and handles many stars, to well-established agencies whose clients you see over and over again on the screen and television, to smaller and smaller agencies who will have maybe only one recognizable name and the rest of whose clients are "day players" who are all very talented and well trained with possibly many years in the business. At the very end of the totem pole are many one-person agencies, where an agent will work out of a small office and does her best to find a one-liner, a walk-on, or such for her unknown clients.

The agencies serve various fields. Every three or four months SAG publishes a list of agents. Next to the name, address, and telephone number of the respective agency, you will find the following letters: *T, C, Y, M*. These letters contain very important information for you.

> *T* stands for *theatrical*. *Film* and *television* are termed theatrical on the West Coast. These agencies will only operate in these areas and will not represent you for stage production.
>
> *C* stands for *commercials*. Agencies followed with the letter *C* will submit you *only* for commercials and nothing else.
>
> *Y* stands for *young people*. These agencies represent infants, children, and teenagers only. Of course if you can play young, you can be a successful "young person" up to your middle twenties.
>
> *M* stands for *modeling*. This means modeling for printwork only, which is photography. Photography includes fashion, magazines, billboards, and so on. It does not include tea room, ramp, or showroom modeling.

Some of the combinations of the letters you may want to familiarize yourself with are the following:

> *T, C*—theatrical and commercial representation
>
> *C, Y, M*—representation of young people for commercials and printwork
>
> *T, C, M*—you guessed it, representation in the fields of television, films, commercials, and printwork

AN INSIDE VIEW INTO
THE WORKINGS OF AN AGENCY

Where do agents come from and how do they submit their clients? Agents come from all the walks of life that are in any way connected to the movie and film industry. Some of the best, kindest, and most knowledgeable agents have been actors themselves at one time or another. They are the agents who will probably forgive you when you come to that first interview with your palms all sweaty as you try to evict that darned frog from your constricted throat. They understand that everyone has to start somewhere. God bless them for that. On the other hand, they are the agents who cannot be fooled and see with a kind of X-ray vision through all of your pretensions, so be completely honest with them.

Some agents have worked as subagents for an agent. They are like an agent's helper, his or her legs so to speak. They were the people who delivered the pictures and résumés to studios, who picked up scripts and called actors in for their interviews. After acquiring some training and knowledge, the subagent might obtain a franchise and open shop on his or her own.

There are former casting directors who have had years of casting experience for major studios and independent productions. They desire to get away from the pressure cooker of studio operation and enjoy the independence of running their own business. These are the kinds of people who can recognize the type they are searching for with their eyes closed. They have developed a sixth sense as far as the camera presence of an actor is concerned and prefer to represent actors who are established or at least well experienced. Once you have gained camera experience, you can never go wrong if a former casting director is interested in representing you.

Some secretaries who have worked for several years at a studio or big agency open their own agencies. These people know the demands of the industry and many people in key positions in the film and television world.

All of these people have several things in common. They all take the business seriously. They have paid their dues to the industry and expect the same from you, the new actor. They are people who are tuned in to the current demands of the industry and the capabilities of the actors they represent. They are not comic strip characters in checkered pants out of some high school play. They also are not gods who can hand you a starring role on a silver platter. They are professionals who have the respect of the industry and demand the same respect and professionalism from their clients. If you work to earn this respect sharpening and developing your acting skills, you will be better equipped to meet the industry's demands, and they in turn will be able to work more effectively in your behalf.

HOW AGENCIES SUBMIT
THEIR CLIENTS

All of the super agencies are involved in packaging. *Packaging* is a term used for grouping stars, well-known director, and screenwriter together. They handle all of these fields and put them together as a "package." A writer writes a screenplay in which a certain star will appear and will be directed by a chosen director. The deals they make add up to millions of dollars.

These big agencies hear about up-and-coming film projects long before anyone else in the industry. Good agents have many contacts; they know producers, directors, and the top casting directors. They are up there where the deals are made during a golf game or at a dinner party. Actors just starting out do need to be concerned with these problems. They will be submitted to a casting director, so let's first discuss the casting process per se.

Casting director A, is an independent, which means she has been hired by a small independent film company to cast their show. She will contact some of the agents that she knows and ask them to submit some actors. Knowing that the producer may go non-union, she will depend primarily on pictures submitted by actors themselves. Soliciting for actors, the casting director will run a *casting notice* in the Hollywood trade *Drama Log* or the New York trade *Back Stage,* then sit back and hold her breath, hoping not to be buried in an avalanche of pictures. She will usually receive about a thousand pictures and will go through them all. Depending on the rightness of type and résumé information, she will call about 10 percent of the actors who submitted themselves. After the initial interview she will have the first *call back,* in which she will ask the actor to read for the part. After this she will have a second call back, in which she will match prospective partners or groups of characters. Possibly the last interview will be taped by video. It is a lengthy process.

Casting director B works for a major studio. He will only deal with top agents. He informs them of his casting requirements by telephone and sometimes personal contact. The entire system of casting for a major film can become very involved as time goes by and if the considerations are not so much the type and ability of the actors but the *name value* domestically and overseas. This is true even for the smaller parts. Other considerations are availability of certain actors, demands as far as billing and fees are concerned, and a thousand minor others.

Casting director C casts television shows and films for larger independent companies. She uses the *breakdown service.* To cast a new pilot, her secretary sends a notice to the breakdown service, giving the name of the show, production company, and names of the producer, director, and casting director. The secretary writes a capsule outline and a list of parts to be cast, giving a description of the characters, which includes their purpose in the story, their age, and sometimes a physical description.

The breakdown, to which agencies all subscribe, is delivered daily, and the agents submit their clients on hand.

Let's say your agent finds a role for you in the breakdown. He has two options. He can take your picture and résumé to the studio where the casting director works, or if he knows the director, he can send in a submission sheet that gives his (the agent's) name, your name, and the show for which you are being submitted. If your agent tells you he has personally delivered your submission to the casting director, it in no way means that he has even spoken to him.

Each big casting office, such as the one at Universal Studios in Hollywood, has a reception area very much like the ones you would see in the dentist's office. Close to the reception desk hovers a box containing various slots on which you see the names of casting directors. Your agent submits you by dropping your submission sheet into the appropriate slot.

At places like Universal the agent also has the opportunity to request to see the scripts of the shows to be cast. This way she or he knows the roles that are coming up in the near future.

Now that we know about submissions, let's visit with casting director C again. Her job is to screen the actors who are submitted to her and sometimes to call agents in order to have certain actors audition. After this she hands to the director "on a silver platter" the names of three or four actors for every part that is open. Casting director C is on contract, and she knows that her contract will only be renewed if she brings in actors who are right for the parts, experienced in front of a camera, and on time. She is not in the business of finding new and exciting talent, because she has not time for this. You must remember, the film industry is a mass medium, not an artistic undertaking. An enormous amount of money rides on each film and television show, and *there is no margin for error.* There is simply no time to let a new, nervous actor repeat his lines several times until he gets them right. There is no patience for lengthy explanations. In short, a television show is no acting class. Once an actor steps before the camera, she or he must be able to perform confidently and securely.

There are casting directors who have discovered new talent, fought for their discoveries, and put their jobs on the line, but these instances are rare. Most casting directors are simply not in a position to do much fighting and are actually standing on one of the lower rungs on the ladder of industry power. They cannot permit themselves to make mistakes and must play it safe. If a casting director is faced with the decision to hire for an unimportant role a mediocre but experienced actor or a newcomer, and say that the newcomer has spark and the mediocre actor is uninspired, he will hire the *safe* actor. He realizes that this spark in the new actor is important, but has no way of knowing how well the new actor will perform in front of the camera. He will also deal with agencies that are established and who have always supplied him with skilled, but not necessarily talented, actors.

The casting directors have to protect their jobs, just like everyone else. If they go out too far on a limb, they will lose their biweekly checks. If they continue to bring in new and exciting actors who lack training and experience and this slows down the shooting, their days at the studio will be numbered.

Now you can see that getting that first role is of prime importance to the new actor. After this first hurdle, each subsequent part will be easier. If you have a solid background in stage training and filmwork and have confidence in yourself and your craft, you will get this first role. It is difficult, but not impossible. In a roundabout way this brings us back to the agent. As you can see, the well-established agent, whether big or small, who can get her clients to read for parts is of great importance. The new agent starting out faces the same difficulties you have to face. He, too, has a frustrating time getting through the casting director's doors. This fact explains the high mortality rate of newly established agencies, which brings us to the next all-important question.

WHICH AGENCY IS BEST FOR YOU?

This is a question that new and established actors ponder over and over again. There are several schools of thought, and each one is right in its own way.

Some actors contend they would only sign with one of the big agencies because

- It gives an actor status to be the client of a large and famous agency.
- Large agencies get the cream of the crop as far as films and television are concerned. The agents know producers and directors personally. The large agencies know even before the breakdown service which shows or films will be cast.
- The large agencies have many agents working for them, and there is always a healthy exchange of roles open for their clients.

Although all of the foregoing holds true, I feel that unknown actors do themselves a disservice by signing with a super agency. Often new actors can get shuffled from agent to agent until they get lost in the hierarchy of such an organization.

Some actors state the benefits of signing with a smaller agency:

- The smaller agents are full of enthusiasm and get-up-and-go. They will burn the midnight oil for you, walk holes in their shoes, or drive holes in their tires to get you a one-day job.

- They will treat you like a human being and not like a product to be bought and sold in the marketplace.

And again, while all of this is true and I could not agree more, the new agents are not yet established, and it is therefore very doubtful that they can get you into a casting director's office to read for a role.

As a new actor you are eager to sign with an agent, but I would like to advise against your signing with a brand-new agency, especially if another more established one is interested in you. An established agent, one who has survived at least two years and has gotten some jobs for her or his clients is much better. If you want to know how long an agency has been in business, just call the agency department of your local Screen Actors Guild office. You do not need to be a member to get this information.

For the actor who already has some credits, the best solution is to look for a small agency whose roster features at least two actors who are fairly well known in the industry, actors who play co-starring roles in films or are regulars on a TV series. Such an agency is highly respected and will be able to get an unknown actor in to read for a part. If such an agency is interested in you, congratulations.

Another factor in selecting an agency is that intangible feeling of friendship and trust. If you sense that the agent is listening to you, understands, and respects the way you see yourself, agrees about the kinds of roles you should be playing, and comes to the phone when you call, then you may be better off with him even if he is a new agency. On the other hand, if you have the distinct feeling that the agent will keep you on the shelf, don't sign with her, no matter how well known she may be. After all, you are a human being, not a product.

HOW TO CONTACT AN AGENT

The first thing to do is to go visit your local SAG office and ask them for a list of franchised agents. As I said, you do not have to be a member to get this information. If there is no SAG office where you live, write to the SAG office in either Hollywood or New York for the one closest to you. If you rely on the Yellow Pages to find an agent, be sure that the agent is franchised by SAG. The SAG office can tell you whether or not an agent is franchised by them.

Remember the various letters behind each agency's name that we discussed a few pages back? Well, now that you have the list of agents, grab a pencil and strike out *all* the agencies featuring only *T* after their name. These are theatrical agencies and will interview only SAG members, so if you are not a SAG member, forget them for right now. But you never know, things may change in the very near future.

Your first targets are the agencies that list an *M* in their combinations of letters—*CM* (commercial and modeling), *TCM* (theatrical, commercial, and modeling)—because with these you can assume that they will see new non-union members. If you are under twenty-one or look under twenty-one, your first target should be an agency listing *Y,* for young people.

As I mentioned before, printwork (*M*) is not under SAG jurisdiction. You do not have to be a member of SAG to do printwork. This is a very beneficial fact for you, the non-union actor. These agencies will most likely want to see you, and if your type is right for them, they might consider signing you. Zooming in on the agencies that handle printwork is the best way to find an agent. Printwork has an enormous turnover of faces, and new faces are always needed. Many actors have comfortably moved from printwork to non-union commercials and from there to union commercials, gotten their SAG cards, and subsequently moved on to film and television work.

Now that you have your agency list marked and your picture and résumé ready, *do not* drop by the agencies to deliver your material. While this practice is common in New York, it is positively frowned upon in Hollywood. Many agencies discourage you openly by displaying a sign on their doors: By Appointment Only. The best thing to do is to telephone the agencies between the hours of 4:00 and 6:00 P.M. only. Your voice should be cheerful and full of energy, without being aggressive. Tell them you *are* an actor. Never admit that you merely *want to be* an actor. Ask them if you might submit a headshot and résumé. They may inquire if you are SAG, and if you are not, it could be the end of the conversation in some cases. They also may ask for your age range, and if they have too many actors in your group, they may decline to accept your picture and résumé.

Don't feel rejected. Just call some more agencies. Be persistent and don't give up. Make a habit of calling different agencies every week. The best days are Tuesday and Wednesday. The rule of thumb is a 10 percent success profile. Out of ten agencies contacted you should get at least one submission. Make a list and write down the names of those you have contacted and the results achieved. Your list of your "actor's bookkeeping" might look like this:

DATE	AGENCY	RESULTS
August 10	ABC Agency	Takes SAG only
" "	DEF Agency	Call back in two mos.
" "	GHI Agency	Send in pix & résumé

The "actor's bookkeeping" is a tool that will make life a little easier for you. After a while it is frustrating trying to remember all the agencies one has contacted.

Sooner than you may imagine, an agency will ask you to send in your materials. Staple your picture and résumé neatly together and attach a *handwritten* note on neat stationery. Keep the note short, businesslike, but casual.
Example:

> Dear Ms. Smith,
>
> Please find attached my picture and résumé, which I am submitting in reference to our recent telephone conversation. Thank you in advance for your kind consideration.
>
> Sincerely

After about five days you should call the agent's office again and ask politely if they have received your materials and if an interview might be arranged. Chances are they have your picture but look at the submissions only once a month, or else they have received it but have too many clients of your type and age range. Or, hopefully, they'll ask you to come in and see them.

At any rate, if they do not invite you to an interview, don't make a pest of yourself by calling again and again. Call the next agent on your list, and eventually you'll get your interview and find an agency that wants to sign you.

However, let's assume that after having contacted about twenty agencies, you have not had one single interview. Then it is time to retrench and search for the faulty link.

The most common faults are the following, in order of frequency:

• Uninteresting, nervous, dull, or aggressive telephone voice. Nerves can play many tricks on people, and your voice, which is normally so melodious, might suddenly change on you as you speak to an agent. Therefore, before you call any more agencies, *practice* these agency calls with your most honest friend and monitor on the other end of the line.

• Pictures. Maybe your headshot is not alive and immediate enough.

• Résumé. Maybe the acting classes you have attended are not impressive enough. Rectify this immediately by trying to get accepted by a well-known workshop or a recognizable coach. Maybe you don't have any screen credits. I am not referring to professional screen credits but to the valuable grad films I've discussed in the chapter on résumés. If you are lacking such grad films, then you are not giving the agent confidence about your ability to work in front of a camera. If for any reason you cannot participate in any grad or thesis films, do enroll in a reputable film school. Maybe you are lacking stage experience. If so, audition for college or community theater productions. At any rate, if you should decide it is your résumé that is holding you back, change this by gaining the training and experience that your résumé obviously lacks.

YOUR CONTRACT WITH AN AGENCY

The all-important moment has arrived: An agency is willing to represent you, and they are going to sign you. Some agents have you sign a SAG as well as an AFTRA contract, even if you are not a member of these unions yet. Don't be disappointed if the agent doesn't have you sign a formal contract. Often agents sign established actors only.

If an agent asks you to bring in twenty-five pictures, then hands you her stationery and asks you to have your résumé photocopied on it, you may rejoice. She has signed you. YOU HAVE AN AGENT.

This informal contract is good for one year. However, SAG has a ruling that if the agent doesn't bring in any *paying* work for you within a three-month period, the contract is null and void and you are free to look for another agency. This is a wise ruling for the at least somewhat established actor. A new actor, on the other hand, should give his agent a six-month period to promote him, because it is difficult to do this in any less time. Give your agent a chance. If she hasn't brought in at least one interview or a reading during a three-month period, then her interest in you may not be very strong. Maybe she has found another actor of your type who has more credits, or perhaps the parts she thought might come up for you didn't materialize. If I were you, I'd start looking for a new agent.

And, believe me, it is so much easier to find the second one. But, a word of advice: As you interview your second agent, do not downgrade your current agency. If asked by a prospective agency why you want to change, NEVER, NEVER say, "I want to change because Ms. Smith has never gotten me work." Simply state that you feel a change of agencies might be beneficial to your career.

THE RELEASE FORM

If an agent signs you or informally agrees to represent you, he or she will hand you a release form. This form states that all monies that you will earn through your agent's efforts will be deposited into the agency account. Most actors balk at this idea, and some have lost good agents because of their refusal to sign.

Believe me when I advise you, DO SIGN. No production company will pay directly to any actor they have hired. Monies are always deposited in the agent's account, and he in turn will write a check to you. There is no danger of loss of money for you; therefore, sign the release. I have never lost one penny by having signed this release.

THE ACADEMY PLAYERS DIRECTORY

Once you have signed with an agent, you are eligible to put your picture as well as the name of your agent into *The Academy Players Directory*. You need not be a member of SAG or AFTRA to be listed in this directory, but you *must have an agent*. This is another reason for getting an agent. *The Players Directory* is published three times a year and is the *bible* of every casting director, agent, and many producers, coast to coast. To have your picture in the directory is a *must*. Many casting directors do not like to keep pictures on file and may only jot down your name and some remarks about your interview or reading. As they look for other actors through the directory, your name and face will become known to them by osmosis. Each issue of the directory comes in two volumes, one devoted to actors (under the headings Juvenile, Leading Man, Character, and Children), the other devoted to actresses (under the headings of Ingenue, Leading Lady, Character, and Children). If you are a comic or a comedienne, you should list yourself as "Character."

THE PERSONAL MANAGER

Actors often ask if they need a personal manager. Personal managers come in many shapes and sizes. There are the star makers, such as Jay Bernstein, who represents such names as Farrah Fawcett, Suzanne Somers, and Linda Evans. Then there are the personal managers who handle a few well-known night club performers. And there are others already mentioned, who take children to auditions. But the rule of thumb is that *if you are a beginning actor, you do not need a personal manager*. If in fact a personal manager should be interested in you, run, don't walk, because you can bet he or she is after your money. No reliable personal manager will take on an unknown, beginning actor. However, if you already have good screen credits and a personal manager of good standing is interested in you, then you should strongly consider her or his services.

Often an actor's career is slowed down because his agent is busy and is not submitting him frequently enough for roles. A personal manager usually never handles more than twenty clients, and since she, just like the agent, receives the breakdown, she can submit her client more often than the agent does or wants to. The personal manager makes it her business to deliver the submission personally and to talk to the casting director and producer. In short, *she makes her client well known.* She will also see that her client has the *right* pictures and the *right* PR.* The personal manager is very closely involved with the actor's career. She receives and fully deserves the 15 to 25 percent of the actor's income that comes from the jobs she has obtained.

The personal manager *cannot negotiate* any acting job for her client. Only the agent is permitted such negotiations. For this reason the actor working with a personal manager should make every effort to see to it that the relationship between the personal manager and the agent is a friendly and trustworthy one. Since personal managers are not SAG franchised, as are agents, the actor thinking of having a personal manager should carefully investigate the personal manager to whom he entrusts himself.

---

*PR is the standard abbreviation for public relations, the kind of general publicity done through pictures and articles in magazines and newspapers.

THE IMPORTANT INTERVIEW

Congratulations, you've signed with an agency. You've made the first hurdle. Someone in this town has recognized you as an *actor*. Someone will submit your pictures and résumé and will actively look for work for you. You might consider giving up your mundane eight-to-five job. After all, you reason, your agent will be setting up interviews for you, and you must be available. Stop. Hold it right there. Take a deep breath before you hand in your resignation. That agent hustling around the studios, lining up readings and interviews for the unknown, but so talented young actor, is a mere phantom created by wishful thinking, an image that has unfortunately found a permanent niche in movies and novels. Such an agent has never existed and will never grace this earth.

True, your agent has signed you, but he will rarely send you out in the beginning. If he is a well-recognized agent with a client list of working actors, the job interviews will go first to those actors who have already brought in work for him. An agent can only make money if his clients bring in the jobs. He, too, has to pay the rent, eat, and put gas in his car.

It is still up to you to further your career. *You* must be the agitating force propelling this new product that is *you the actor*. The first step you must take is the *general interview*. The general interview is designed merely for the purpose of meeting with various casting directors and establishing, hopefully, a contact for the future, that is, "getting a foot in the door." Only in rare cases, and only if the actor has impressive credits, will an agent set up general interviews with a casting director. It is up to *you* the actor to introduce yourself to the casting directors.

76

It is called an *interview* when you are actually being considered for a part, along with fifty other lucky actors. You'll only chat with the casting director, since in film production, the *reading* will follow the interview. For a television show, and especially if time is at a premium, you will read immediately for the part. Once you've done the reading, you'll wait and pray for a *call back*. Most likely at the call back you will be reading for the casting director, the director, the producer, and possibly the writer. Sometimes one call back will suffice. If you are up for a fairly important role, at least a featured part, you might have to live through a number of call backs as the choice narrows down more and more. If you are a member of SAG, the production company for whom you are auditioning will have to pay you after the second call back.

All in all, you'll find such interviews for film and television to be a pleasant experience. Enjoy them and make the best of them. The *cattle call*, by contrast, is a degrading experience, in which hundreds of actors are auditioned and you have to wait for hours to be seen. This practice is still very, very much in vogue as far as stagework is concerned, but has all but been eliminated in the film industry. Thanks to SAG, the actor is now given an appointment and seldom has to wait very long to be seen.

THE CASTING DIRECTOR'S POSITION IN FILM AND TELEVISION

Before going on to a detailed discussion regarding the various interviews, we might first consider the casting director's position in the film business.

Looking realistically at the casting director's position, we must admit that it encompasses a wide variety of power levels. If, as happens frequently in small independent companies, the director as well as the producer are involved in the casting process from the very beginning, then the casting director might be nothing more than a glorified secretary. On another level, there are others whose casting decisions are major contributions to the final result of the film or television show. I know of various television projects in which director and producer will trust their highly experienced and creative casting director so implicitly that they do not even meet the actors until they show up on the set on the day of shooting.

Generally speaking, the quality of the efforts casting directors make toward the projects they are casting and the actors who are being considered have much to do with their talent and perception. They must sense what the producers and directors envision as they present talent to the upper echelon.

The actor who reads for a part must remember that the casting director has to answer to the director, the director has to answer to the producer, and the producer has to answer to the studio or network. This explains why casting directors are really not so free in their choices, but must "second-guess" what everyone else wants. This in turn usually leads to the casting of "known commodities," actors who have established solid track records. They are not necessarily actors of outstanding talent, but they come in on time, know their lines, and are able to perform before the camera.

THE GENERAL INTERVIEW

First you should send in your picture and résumé to various casting directors. You can get a list from your local SAG office, but remember that this list will very quickly become obsolete, because independent casting directors move from job to job. One season a certain casting director might be casting for a television show and the next season for some independent films. You should make it a practice to get a new list every three months in order to be up to date.

Send your materials to every casting director listed. After all, you want to get your face and name known. It is true that in the beginning of your career you may feel more like a mail order salesperson than an actor. It is also true that most of your pictures will end up in the wastebasket. So what? If only a few of your pictures catch a casting director's attention and bring you a general interview, your mail campaign will have been a success.

Once you have mailed out your initial batch of pictures and résumé, you will want to follow it up by giving the casting director a call. You *don't* have to have an agent or be a member of SAG to request a *general interview*, since casting directors will see actors who do not have union affiliation. Do not insist on speaking directly to the casting directors, but ask if they will accept pictures and a résumé in reference to a general interview.

Once you have been given the green light, sit down and write a short handwritten note of pleasant tone and polite informality. Never begin your note with "Hi." Nor should you address the casting director by his or her first name. Remember, this is a business letter, not a personal note. An acceptable letter might read like this:

> Dear Ms. Castwell,
>
> Attached please find my picture and résumé, which I am submitting in reference to a possible general interview. I shall call your office within the next few days to ask if I

may be seen by you. Thank you in advance for your kind consideration.

Sincerely,

Rick Actor

Please use plain white notepaper of good quality. Cutesy notes displaying cat or flower designs should be kept for friends and are in poor taste for business letters. You may choose to have your name printed on the note-paper, since it would give the letter a personal touch. *Staple* this note to the picture and résumé. Remember, too, that the picture and résumé must also be stapled together.

Make certain that you are sending your best 8-by-10-inch head-shot. It doesn't have to be the most glamorous, but it should be the one that is most full of *vitality* and that *resembles you the most.* If you send in a headshot that is misleading, then you will be taking your first wrong step and you will miss out on parts that are right for you.

Some actresses consistently send in the wrong kinds of headshots. Very young actresses, not realizing that youth and vitality are their keys to success, will too often be tempted to send in a sophisticated or sexy-looking photo. There are also actresses who have passed their fortieth birthday who hang on for dear life to the looks they had when they were an ingénue. What's so wrong with a wrinkle here or there? We are all getting older, right? There are so many exciting roles for the middle-year actress that this lady should not try to hide the candles on her cake, but should go out for the roles that are right for her age range.

The headshot that will get you that general interview is the one that shows the advertised product, *you,* as you really are. If a headshot exudes the reality of you and your personality, then age and looks are only secondary.

Making contact by telephone is mandatory in Hollywood. You never "just drop by" at a casting director's office or a production company asking to be seen. This of course makes it difficult for an actor to be seen in an interview. However, contrary to Hollywood, it is perfectly all right to "make the rounds" in New York. You may leave your picture and résumé at the casting director or production company's front office. If you can make friends with the secretary, you may even have a better chance of seeing someone. You may not get an interview the first time that you visit the office, but eventually you will meet the casting director. The custom of making the rounds in New York may be bad for your shoes, but it's great for your soul. You'll have the feeling of being active and more involved in your career as you visit the casting offices and commercial agents. New York is the hub for television commercials, so the beginning actor would do well to establish as many contacts as possible with casting directors and commercial agents. They have enormous files with thousands of pictures and résumés that are all categorized by types. Since these commercial agents are *not signing* talent, but are free-lancing, your chances of being called in for a commercial interview are much greater if you are listed with as many commercial agents as possible. Since they see so many pictures, though, you should make a continuous effort to keep up the contact with these agents. Do remind them that you are "still alive and kicking."

Make it a habit to drop by every so often for a friendly chat, but keep it short. (Remember that the agent and his or her secretary are busy and they have work to do.) When agents are able to associate the face on the photo with the person they have met and remember, your chances of getting called in are much better.

HOW TO DRESS
FOR YOUR GENERAL INTERVIEW

Soon the important day arrives and you are ready to go on your general interview. You stand in front of the mirror and ponder the question, "What shall I wear?" The only rule of thumb is to wear something in which you feel comfortable, as long as it is clean and attractive. Arriving unshaven or in an outfit in dire need of washing and pressing doesn't stamp you as a gifted actor, but only shows that you are a sloppy one. It doesn't glorify you as a talented actress if your hair is stringy and you need a manicure. Your negligence about your appearance is simply a mark of carelessness that might carry over into your acting. Most of all, avoid the affected "actor's look" of torn T-shirt and jeans. There is nothing wrong with wearing a T-shirt and jeans as long as they are clean and neat. If you fall into the ingenue or juvenile category, then you should avoid getting dressed up. That is to say, if you are uncomfortable wearing an outfit that you don't usually wear, it might be difficult to be your relaxed, vivacious self.

If you fall within the leading lady or character category, an outfit of casual chic is best. Fad fashions should be avoided at all cost, since your outfit should not draw so much attention that it overshadows you. For this reason, don't wear an abundance of jewelry. You should shine, not your bracelets or rings. Each piece of jewelry is only justified if it compliments *you* and is but one segment of the entire picture that you present.

Take a good look at your hair style. Is your hair professionally styled? Does it bring out your best features? You should wear your hair simply but attractively styled. An elaborate evening hairdo is as much out of place as elaborate makeup. There is nothing worse than seeing an actress at 10:00 A.M. in full evening battle makeup.

Actors have it somewhat easier than actresses when they dress for a general interview. First of all, male fashions are far less distracting, more simple and straightforward. The garments draw less attention than anything created for women. The actor who falls into the leading man or character category should make an effort to express clearly the *type* he wants to project. The healthy outdoors type should not wear a blue suit for the interview, and a loud checkered sport jacket would prove equally distracting. The outdoors type would look the best in a simple sport coat as well as turtleneck sweater and color-coordinated slacks. If you are an intellectual or executive type, then the dark blue or gray suit will literally "suit" you. Beware of the tie; your best choice for an interview is a solid color or one that has a small pattern. Avoid bold stripes and contrasting designs, because they will draw attention away from your face. Keep your jewelry simple and small.

As you select the interview outfit, ask yourself the following questions:

- Is the outfit right for the type I wish to convey?
- Is the outfit right for my age?
- Is the outfit right for my figure type?
- Do I feel comfortable and attractive?

MEETING THE CASTING DIRECTOR

Now that all the preliminaries are out of the way, you go to your general interview. As you sit in the waiting room, you should remind yourself of the things that the interview *is not:*

- It is not the place to be discovered. If your hopes run in this direction, you should find another profession in which to make a living. Very rarely do actors get discovered, and if something like that does happen, they become an "overnight discovery" only after many years of hard work in their profession.
- It is not the place to air grievances about the industry, the scarcity of acting jobs, the difficulty of getting into SAG. Yes, these are all problems, but keep your mouth shut in the casting office and do your complaining at home to your cat or dog.
- This is not the place to ask for advice about your acting career. Casting directors do not run "Dear Abby" columns.

Fully realize that the general interview is just an occasion to introduce yourself to the industry and to various casting directors. Enjoy the interview, enjoy this first step that you take toward participating in this marvelous institution we call the movie industry. You've got your foot in the door, be proud and happy about that.

As you are waiting to be seen, don't use this time to participate in an animated conversation with the other actors waiting with you. Remember that this is a place of business and you are here for a business appointment, not a social call. Don't pester the secretary with questions about what show is being cast, who will be in it, and so on. Don't distract him from his work, but do be friendly and polite. A secretary is an important person, so don't treat him like a piece of furniture. He cannot help you with your interview, but more than one secretary has moved on to be casting assistant, then to casting director, and some even to heads of talent departments. You never know what can happen in the future, and if you are friendly to this person behind the typewriter, it could be important for you later on.

Another reason why you shouldn't engage in conversations with other actors is that such jabbering can diminish your energy, and you may lose all of the vitality that you'll need later on in the interview. Just sit quietly and breathe deeply if a flutter of nervous energy threatens to overcome you. Remind yourself that a general interview is nothing more than a friendly chat and that there is no reason for you to be nervous.

Remind yourself that this is not the first interview that you've been through. Several years ago you interviewed for a baby-sitting job, you interviewed for MacDonald's and at the dime store on Main Street. You've always been relaxed and friendly, right? People like you, right? So what's so different now? You'll come across more impressively if you are relaxed and confident about yourself. Casting directors agree that actors would do better if they took the interview more like an everyday job interview rather than a matter of life and death.

Now the secretary calls your name and you are ushered in to see the casting director. You walk in proudly, smile, look at him and shake his hand. Simple? Yes, very simple. You will be surprised to learn that many an interview has gone sour because the talented and well-trained actor was nervous and didn't show confidence.

Even though you have mailed in your picture and résumé, it's a good idea to carry an extra one with you to hand to the casting director after the introduction. Sit relaxed and attentive. If the casting director wants to see your portfolio, don't interrupt her or him by jabbering about your credits. Let her look at the photos and read the résumé. If she has any questions, she will ask. As you answer, be positive about yourself without bragging. On the other hand, don't sell yourself short. If you are a fairly good tennis player and the casting director asks you about this ability, do not reply modestly, "Somewhat," but say, "Yes, I am quite experienced." Show that you are proud of your accomplishments, no matter how insignificant they may seem to you. If you are a beginner, don't be afraid to admit that you've had no professional work, but be proud of everything that you have done, including your stagework at college and/or community theaters. And don't forget the grad and thesis films as credits. This attitude encourages enthusiasm in the casting director. Be enthusiastic about yourself, your life in general, and this interview in particular. Stress your good qualities, don't discuss your problems, and, let me repeat this, don't apologize for your lack of professional credits.

Most casting directors are not only good conversationalists, they genuinely like people. Help them to get to know you, discuss all kinds of topics, such as what your hometown is like, how you feel about some topical subject, or your favorite hobby. Of course, there are some casting directors who are not brilliant conversationalists, and if you are sitting opposite one of these, then it is up to you to break the ice. Look around the office and find something that immediately attracts your attention. It could be a poster, an antique, a gadget, some green plants, or whatever might give you a clue to what the casting director's hobby might be. Point out this item by talking about it, and soon both of you will enjoy your little chat.

Last, but not least, take a good look at your *human* qualities. Let's face it, you are first a person, only second an actor. Your own personality is the final deciding point when you are being considered for a role. You have to sell this personality during the interview, you must *light up, be animated* and *enthusiastic,* yet at the same time not push or put up a false front. You must be natural, be yourself. I'll admit that it's not an easy order to fill. Acting is a topic that should be avoided at all cost. Do not talk about acting in general, and especially do not "wax gleefully" in praise of your favorite acting technique.

"Why?" you will probably ask. "I know quite a bit about acting. I have taken acting classes, and I have performed, so why not show the casting director how knowledgeable I am about the subject?" Unfortunately most actors are "onstage" when they discuss acting; they are not themselves; they become actors spelled with a capital *A.* Since your own personality is the key factor to success, *you must be you* during the interview. I hope that I've made my point and that you'll avoid discussing acting techniques.

Use the general interview to acquaint the casting director with your likable natural self, the actor who is secure and confident. Avoid all nervous mannerisms, since it could tip him off to your insecurities.

- Don't fidget in your chair
- Don't play with your hair or jewelry
- Don't rub your hands or clench your fingers
- Don't tap your foot
- Don't clear your throat before speaking

THE FOLLOW-UP

After about fifteen or twenty minutes your interview is ended. You thank the casting director for his time, you tell him that it was nice to meet with him and that you enjoyed the chat. The interview is now over. That's it. You scratch this particular casting director off your list, since you have now seen him, talked with him, and hopefully made a good impression. You have no more responsibilities.

Wrong. Your responsibilities concerning this general interview have just begun. You've got your foot in the door, and now it is up to you to keep this door open. You must keep your *name* and *face* in the casting director's memory. The first step to take is to write a short friendly note. At the time you ordered your composites, you also ordered a healthy supply of postcards, showing your trademark picture and your name. This is the card you will use for your thank-you note.

You will have to remind the casting director of your existence every so often, and the best way to do this is to send these little postcards every six weeks or so to let him know how you are doing in your career. You may have joined a workshop or another acting class taught by a new coach or conducted at a college, got new pictures, have been cast in a play or student film. Let the casting director know that you are still alive and kicking and actively pursuing your career. After you have landed a professional job or commercial, be sure to let him know. *Do not* call the casting director; don't ever call, since you will only speak to his secretary. Many actors who have kept up their mailing lists to casting directors have gotten their first role this way. Keeping this in mind, you can easily see how important it is to be seen in as many general interviews as possible.

Be sure to keep track of all of your interviews. Write down every interview that you have had, dating and recording the results. Honestly evaluate how well you did and how you might improve. Ask yourself the following questions:

- Was I my vibrant self, or did I assume some phony or pushed personality?
- Was I enthusiastic about myself and my accomplishments?
- Did I talk too much or too little?

- Did I feel comfortable, or was I nervous?
- Did I really listen to what the casting director was saying?

DRESSING ACCORDING TO CHARACTER

You've had several general interviews, you've faithfully kept up your mailings, and now, frightfully soon, the impossible happens—your agent calls you in for a reading.

"Hello," he says, "you have an interview tomorrow at eleven at Universal. You are to read for John Castwell for the part of Alice, a college student. Good luck. Call me right after the reading and tell me how it went."

First you faint. That's all right, after all it's your first *professional reading*. Immediately after you've recovered from the initial shock, you'll call your agent back and ask her or him specifics about the part. Hopefully she'll be able to enlighten you about the age, disposition, and looks of the character. After all, she has the breakdown sheet handy. She'll say, "All right, here we have Alice. As I said before, she is a college student. She's a friendly and helpful woman, plain-looking, and she has one scene."

Your first concern is how you should dress to make yourself believable as Alice. You look into your mirror. Well, you're no ravishing beauty, but you are rather attractive. Quickly you decide to go to the interview without makeup and wear the dowdiest, most ill-fitting outfit you own.

Wrong. They write "plain" in the breakdown sheet, but usually they cast "pretty." This means that you should look attractive when you walk in to the casting director's office. You shouldn't look like this year's sexpot or last season's glamor queen, but you should come in dressed neat and attractive in an outfit that stresses your good points. Your hairdo and makeup should be simple but flattering. Got it?

So that it might give added believability to the role, you should try to dress *somewhat* like the character that you are to portray. The producer, director, and casting director often have preconceived ideas about the part, and this will help you. A tailored skirted suit is appropriate if you are up for the part of an executive or lawyer, but it is wrong if you are reading for the part of a waitress. A cheerful cotton dress would be more in keeping with the vision in the casting director's mind. Of course, no one would expect you to waltz in wearing a hoopskirt if you were up for the part of Martha Washington.

A suit and tie would be appropriate for the role of a clergyman rather than a sport shirt and jeans. By the same token, if you read for the part of a lumberjack, don't confuse the casting director by wearing slacks and a turtleneck sweater.

Some casting directors insist that you dress for the part, while others don't care one way or the other. Ask your agent about this particular casting director's view on the matter. If your agent is unable to give you this information, then give the casting director's secretary a call, as she may be able to enlighten you.

Actresses often ask whether jeans are appropriate when reading for a part. Some women look absolutely fantastic in jeans, whereas others do not really look their best. There are times when slacks are just about the most perfect thing to wear, but unfortunately some actresses use slacks to cover their legs, because, let's say, these would not exactly win a beauty contest. It's embarrassing for a casting director to ask about the looks of your legs, and such a question could be interpreted as sexual harassment. The casting director might like your reading, but might cast another actress who had the foresight to wear a skirt for the reading, thus assuring the casting director that she was not ashamed of her legs. For this reason, it's better to wear a skirt or dress for an audition or reading. Yet, if you feel that pants would add believability to the part, then by all means wear them. However, at the same time do carry a picture in your portfolio that will prove to the casting director the fine state of your legs.

Generally it is best to avoid busy patterns. Choose solid colors whenever possible, since solids give a strong immediate impact. The colors you should avoid at all cost for interviews are *kelly green* and *purple*. Psychological studies have shown that these two colors cause uneasiness in the person viewing you. These colors are overpowering in themselves and tend to obliterate the person wearing them.

Usually your agent will call you a day ahead of the interview, but it also might happen that he calls you a few hours prior to the appointment. Therefore, make it a habit to have your hair and clothes ready at all times. It might be a good idea to save one or two outfits for interviews only.

PREPARING FOR YOUR READING

After this long, but necessary detour, let's get back to the *reading*. Your interview has been scheduled for 2:00 P.M. Leave home early, allowing time for traffic congestion and for finding the casting director's office. If your reading is at a studio, you might be faced with the fact that you are not allowed to park on the lot. This means that you must park outside and will have to walk to the office. You should also consider that the casting director's office may be hard to find and be situated in some obscure building. Most studios are a maze of sound stages and buildings large and small. They may remind you of an unsolvable jigsaw puzzle, as you search frantically for Mr. Castwell, the casting director for the Nowhere Company, who is presently casting the epic horror movie *The Guppie Attacks Hong Kong*. Make a point of arriving at the casting office about thirty minutes early. This gives you time to freshen up and relax for a moment before you tackle your script. Yes, work on your script. Simply reading the scene and then putting it down, confidently but foolishly relying on your personality and good looks, is not enough. Many actors get in the habit of doing just that. If you are to be seen by a casting director whom you have already met, remember that you are being called in, first, because you are the type he wants and second because he likes your personality. Now it is up to you to convince him that you not only have a terrific, vital personality but the talent and craft to back it up.

Most likely you will see the script and scene for which you will be reading on the day of the reading. Sometimes there is a chance to pick up the script at the studio *before* your scheduled appointment, but don't bank on it. However, if you are up for a featured or co-starring role, you should insist on seeing the script at least a day ahead of the reading. There is a SAG ruling to this effect, so make full use of it by picking up the script prior to the audition. Don't be afraid that you may impose upon the casting office— picking up your script is a sign of your reliability as an actor.

"Cold" readings for film and television are far more difficult than reading for a stage play. If you are auditioning for a known play, then you can always get a copy of the play at a library or book store. By the time you audition, you may not only be completely familiar with the play but will have been able to work on your part. Even if you are auditioning for an unpublished play, you will sometimes have the opportunity to familiarize yourself with your part prior to the audition.

In any case you will have considerably more text at your disposal than if you are reading for a film, and this in itself makes stage reading less complicated. Stage actors who read for the first time for a television show are shocked by how little text they have to work with. Feature films, by their nature, are more visually oriented than television and are therefore even more economical as far as text is concerned. Yet, cold readings are a fact of life for screen actors and a hurdle they must take if they are to survive in the business. I would advise all actors to take a good cold-reading class. The money spent for such a class is well invested and will pay dividends over and over again.

As you enter the reception room, you will find that the secretary has a stack of scripts or scenes on his or her desk. You will give him your name and, if you are a member of SAG, your SAG number. You will then tell him the name of the character for which you are reading, and if you are reading at a big studio like Universal, it is good to let him know the name of the casting director and show.

SELLING YOUR READING

Many factors go into casting decisions besides good looks, personality, talent, and craft. All of these factors are out of your control, but if your readings are interesting and dynamic, eventually you will be cast, even if you lose out on many parts. For this reason, you must *give your all* at every reading.

Keep this thought in mind as you enter the casting director's office. As you close the door behind you, you should realize that the person behind the desk is not your enemy. In fact, this man or woman is just as eager as you are to see you succeed. You want the part and she or he wants the best actor to fill the role. It is as uncomplicated as that. For this reason, do not put the casting director and later the director on a level of power above you. Whether you are a beginner or a seasoned actor, *you* are the controlling force during the reading. You are the important person in the office at this moment, not the casting director. Knowing that you are the controlling force will keep you from the self-defeating attitudes of hostility and servility. Knowing that you can and will *control* will give the casting director confidence in you. Let your self-assurance, your energy, and your intelligence come through from the first moment on.

If the part for which you are reading seems diametrically opposed to your personality and you wonder why in heaven they called you for the role, then cleverly try to do your reading as soon as possible. If you sneak your personality up on the casting director *while* you are reading, you have an excellent chance of selling her on the idea that yours is the personality she really wants.

In any case it's best not to draw the casting director into any lengthy conversations. If she has any questions as to your background and credits, keep your answers brief and to the point. Also keep your own questions in regard to the part for which you are reading short. If something is unclear in the scene, have it explained, by all means. You may even let her know—and every casting director will be delighted to hear this—that you have different interpretations for the scene, but refrain from analyzing the role to pieces, since you will talk yourself right out of a role with the speed of lightning.

If you must have a moment of preparation, take it, but refrain from such self-defeating mannerisms as rolling your head or shoulders, clenching and unclenching your fists, and to top off the lists of *don'ts,* don't cough. Please don't clear your throat, even if you know that the granddaddy of all frogs has taken up residence in there. Let me remind you that none of these mannerisms serves any purpose, they don't relax you, and they clearly warn the casting director of your insecurities. You should give her the confidence that you are able to do the part and that she will hire a secure actor if she casts you.

As you begin reading, don't read *blandly*. No one expects you to give a finished performance, but since you are competing with many actors, the one who gives the most interesting and alive interpretation will usually be the one who is cast. If you read blandly, or in kinder words, "laid back," your chances of getting a call back are slim. Sometimes the most conscious actors are the ones who bring in bland cold readings. They are so concerned about the "rightness" of the scene and that the scene make sense, that they forget *why* they are in the casting director's office. They are not there to direct the scene, but to be cast for the part. Whether a scene is done correctly and in unity with the rest of the script is the director's responsibility, not theirs. The actor's responsibility is to read in such a way as to sell himself as an actor.

This means you must convey your own personality and vitality and combine that with a *colorful* interpretation of the character. Whether this interpretation is close to how the director sees it and how later he wants to have the scene played is immaterial. You have no way of knowing how the director wants to shoot this scene, and since you are familiar only with *this* scene, you have no way of knowing what happened before and what will happen next in the script. This may be important information for you to know in order to interpret the scene sensibly, but these two important factors—not knowing what the director wants and having no knowledge of the entire script—often draw actors into doing a "safe" reading. That is, they will read blandly and without interest, since they are afraid of bringing in a "wrong" interpretation.

Never, ever ask or worry about "how they want it." How they want it is completely immaterial at this point in the cold reading. They will let you know what they want when they call you in on a call back. At your first reading you should only be concerned about showing yourself as the exciting, interesting actor you are and as a good possible choice for the part to be cast. All this lengthy discussion means is that *you must sell your cold reading*. Never read blandly, monotonously, or uninterestingly.

Selling a cold reading boils down to three points to remember: energy, communication, and spontaneity. We will discuss each one in turn.

Energy

As you know energy comes on various levels. You, the actor must be astute enough, not only to gauge the energy level of the character you are portraying, but also the *general energy level* of the TV or film for which you are reading. This is fairly easy. If you have seen the show often enough, you will have absorbed the energy level of this particular show into your subconscious. If you are reading for a feature film or a pilot, you might feel in limbo, but you really aren't. There is a rule of thumb to follow in dealing with energy levels.

Let's assume you are reading for an action series or an action horror film. Remember that in both genres the actors are secondary to the action or horror. The actors are *part of an action*: Cars may be crashing, guns are being fired. If you *overact,* you are entirely out of the concept of the show. Tone your acting down, act simply and believably. In no way permit yourself to become bland or monotonous. Your acting must be colorful, you have to be yourself, you have to communicate and be interesting, but notch your acting down. If you are reading for a *dramatic show* or *soap opera,* or any of the many film and television shows dealing with human emotions, simply read on your energy level, that is to say the level *you as the actor* are most comfortable in. However the picture changes completely if you are reading for any of the sitcoms (situation comedy). Here *top energy level* is the rule. In comedy the focus is completely on you the actor. There is no action otherwise. If in doubt, give a little more energy, never less. If you give more, they know they can tone you down. But never confuse *high* energy with overacting. Even in comedy you must strive to be simple and believable.

Communication

Communication means to get your point across to the other person. Communication, this aura of naturalness and alertness, is what every casting director demands, and if he finds these qualities in an actor, he will seriously consider him for the part.

All day long as you live and breathe, you are communicating with someone or something. Yes, "something" too, for you scream at your typewriter ribbon if it sticks, you call your purse a name when it has the offending habit of disappearing into nowhere when you are in a rush to get to an audition—in fact, you are always communicating. You communicate with another person when you listen to what she is saying, you react to her opinion, then finally you try to get your point across. It's simple to communicate in everyday life, and it's also fairly simple as you do a scene, even though you know in advance what the other person's response will be.

Communication becomes more difficult to handle when you cold-read. Let's discover where the difficulties lie and find some ways of overcoming them.

The first and most obvious reason why it is difficult for the actor to achieve this communication is the hard and cold fact that communication is between two people. It is a give and take that you won't likely find as you are reading opposite a casting director. You will get little or no reaction from this person sitting across the desk from you. Giving it some thought, you cannot blame the casting director for this lack of dramatic impact. First of all, the deadpan delivery of his lines in no way means a lack of interest in you. It might mean that the casting director has read those lines during the past few days ad nauseam and will be reading them over and over again for the remainder of the week. He is literally burnt out. Also, the more blandly he reads, the better he can concentrate on *your* interpretation. Primarily the reason for the casting director's bland delivery, then, is his need to pay attention to your interpretation. He is careful not to control the scene himself, because if he were to do so, he might lead you away from your own interpretation. By reading his line without emotion, he in fact turns the *control* of the scene over to you.

Therefore, do not fall into the trap of delivering your lines equally as blandly and unemotionally, thinking that this is what the casting director wants. Rushing is another one of the signs of inexperienced actors. The moment such actors step into the casting director's office, they have the desire to get the reading over with as quickly as possible. If they are asked why they are in such a rush, the predictable answer is, "I didn't want to take up too much time."

Nonsense, you are in the casting director's office because he thinks you might fit the role. No one has held a gun to his head; he asked his secretary to call your agent. You are in his office because he wants you to be there, so take *sufficient time* for your reading. Rushing never pays off; it only shows your insecurity, which, as you know, is a dangerous mark against you.

Spontaneity

In life you are always spontaneous, whether you know it or not, because you don't know exactly what will happen within the next few seconds. For this reason you have to *listen*, you have to *react* to a given situation, and you have to *think*. Yet, during a reading many actors lose this spontaneity because they know in advance what their partner or casting director's response will be and because they know the outcome of the scene. All these components easily push an actor into a rushing and monotonous performance. In order to achieve spontaneity you must step on your mental brakes and slow down your cold reading. Listen as you would listen in real life, as if you were hearing the casting director's lines for the first time, and then react. Most importantly, give yourself time to think. In life you often think before you speak. Observe yourself as you relate some incident to a friend or as you argue with her about some matter and you will notice that you always think. You might give some thought before you speak or after you have made a statement. Very often you may stop in the middle of a sentence for a moment of reflection before you go on, but no matter what, you always think.

If you apply the same technique in your cold readings, you will never lack spontaneity.

THE CALL BACK

A *call back* is a second reading of the role, which means that you have been accepted into the charmed circle of those "chosen" the ones who are being considered for the part. For smaller TV parts you will usually read only twice, once for the casting director and the second time for the director, producer, and possibly the writer. If the production company is in the middle of shooting and you are up for a bit part, they will notify your agent the very evening of the reading, at latest the next day, but usually there will be about three to six days before you could be called in for a call back. If you are up for a more substantial part, let's say a feature part, you will probably have at least two call backs. If you are up for a feature film at a major studio or a large independent company or for a nationwide commercial, the call backs could be numerous.

But we are getting ahead of ourselves. After your initial reading and before you leave the office, ask the secretary if you might take the scene with you to study. Sometimes, your request will be granted, if not, you may want to jot your lines down.

For the call back, keep the same interpretation that you gave at the cold reading, changing only if the casting director suggests some change. Don't discard what you first presented at the casting office, since *this is what they liked.* Work on the script, dig yourself into the part, strengthen your interpretation, but do not change it.

Many actors ask a coach to work with them on their lines. If the coach knows you, has worked with you extensively before, and respects your personality and interpretation, then to ask his help is a wise decision. But, if the coach that you choose primarily works on audition material, then I doubt whether such coaching would be to your benefit. Such a coach would not be familiar with your personality, and since your own interpretation of the scene is not completely worked out, he might change the interpretation to such an extent that it will be unrecognizable from the scene you presented in the casting office. Remember, they called you back because they liked your first reading.

Wear the same outfit that you wore for the first reading. The casting director has formed a mental picture of you that she liked. *Do not* change it in any way. Yes, if you wore jeans and a T-shirt for your first reading because it was a sweltering day, wear the same thing for the call back, even if the temperature has dropped and everyone else is sporting turtleneck sweaters.

Well, here you are again in the reception room, waiting to read. After a few minutes the casting director will emerge from her office, shake hands, make small talk, then take you to the producer's office. Again you'll find a waiting room and a busy secretary. You wait, wait, and wait again. You'd better get used to it because waiting is much of what this business is about. Finally you will be ushered into the producer's office. The casting director will introduce you to a group of people, among them the writer and director, plus some assorted faces, whose names and positions are rather vague to you at this moment. Without further preliminaries you will be asked to read. Again the casting director will be reading opposite you. By this time you know your lines perfectly, but it's still better to keep the script in your hands, since you never know when your memory might give out under pressure. Be relaxed and take it easy.

As you read, keep yourself focused on the casting director. Do not look around, directing various lines to various people in the room. You are not giving a public speech, you are having a conversation with another person, the casting director. You do not have to cater to others, and if you do, you will fragment your reading. If the director likes your reading, he might ask you to change a few things, to read this or that line differently. This is not a putdown of your interpretation. He only wants to see whether or not you can be "directed." Even though you have worked on the role extensively, familiarized yourself with the part, and formed a concept of your own, give yourself enough room to change if the director suggests a change. *Do not* "lock yourself" into your own interpretation.

Sooner than you think, just as you have begun to enjoy your call back, it will be ended. Everyone thanks you politely, assuring you that they liked your reading, and next thing you know you are out of the office, out of the building, out of the front gate, and on your way home. Again the waiting begins. You may or may not get the part, no matter how good your reading or how right your type and personality. These are some of the facts to be considered in the process of casting. We will discuss them at length later.

THE COMMERCIAL INTERVIEW

Last but not least is the commercial interview, which is probably the most difficult to master. A commercial is on the air thirty seconds at the most. This means that you have no time to establish your character. You must establish your character within the first five or ten seconds of the commercial. While it may seem that the advertising firm that has commissioned and is paying for the commercial is selling a product, what they are really selling is *you,* the type, the person. Remember what we said about *commercial identity* in a previous chapter? Please keep commercial identity in mind as you go out to read for commercials. In no other field is *type* so important as in the commercial. Next to type, *energy and vitality* are the determining factors in the decision as to whether or not you will be cast for a particular commercial.

Usually you will be handed just a few lines of text, unless it's a commercial in which only your reaction is important and you have no text to handle. But let's assume that you have some lines to speak. Looking at these few sentences, you might think, "Easy as pie." Wrong. To deliver these few lines is a far more complex and difficult job than were many long scenes that you have done.

Basically commercials come in two categories, hard sell and soft sell. In *hard sell* commercials a high energy level is required. Many comedy commercials fall into this category. *Soft sell* commercials, on the other hand, approach the public in a soft and subtle manner. Most beauty products, such as perfume, lipstick, and shampoo, are soft sell.

Both types of commercial are trying to put forward one or more of the following ideas:

- Benefit (what you can gain by using the product)
- uniqueness of product
- Dream (if owned, the product will fulfill a dream of yours)

Understanding which one of these categories your commercial falls in is easy if you are dealing with luxury items such as cars, boats, perfumes, or diamonds, for these very obviously fall into the dream category. They make viewers feel that if they buy this car, they will attract the type of glamorous woman seen standing beside the car or that if they buy this certain brand of coffee, their partner will look as lovingly at them as the actor on the screen is looking at the actress. And so on and so on, you've got the idea.

To define uniqueness is a little harder, because basically as soon as something is advertised for the mass market, it is not really unique anymore. But even so a mundane product as detergent can stress the uniqueness of this *particular* kind of detergent.

Most commercials fall into the benefit category. This covers everything from canned peaches to tires.

Once you have recognized the category of the commercial you are reading for, find those lines in the text that stress the category. These are the lines that you will make the most important in your delivery. *These lines must stand out, must sell.*

As you go in to read for the commercial, you might encounter two different situations. You will either read for a casting director or your reading will be taped. Your interview will not take longer than five or ten minutes at the most. A very short time to sell your talent and definitely not enough time to make any mistakes. Tough? Right, very tough, unless you are well trained and possess "right-away power," the most important quality the commercial actor needs besides commercial identity.

Most commercial casting directors break right-away power down into the following components, and you might as well be aware of them:

- Do smile
- Be animated
- Show vitality
- Communicate in a conversational way

Remember, you have to display *all* of these qualities within the first five seconds of the commercial.

This right-away power should in no way be something phony, but should flow from your own self, from a force of inner energy.

As mentioned before, you will most likely be taped. Even if a commercial is cast and produced in Los Angeles, it is likely that the advertising firm commissioning the commercial will be located in New York. This is why most commercial interviews are taped. Most tapes will be shot on ¾-inch color tape, and for this reason you should avoid any black or white in your outfit, and stay away from showy jewelry, dominantly printed scarfs, or wild belts. A simple solid-colored outfit is best.

If you are doing a union commercial, SAG requires that cue sheets be placed both to the right and to the left of the camera. If you are doing a non-union commercial, no such regulation exists, and you will read from copy.* Do not try to memorize the text of your commercial. No one requests it of you or expects you to know your text. True, you'll have only a few lines to remember and you'll probably know them by heart once you step in front of the camera, but if you are new in this business, you never know when your nerves will play tricks on you, so hold on to your copy for dear life. They will not give you a "dry run" on camera but will rather tape your reading immediately, then say, "Thank you, next please," and your audition is over.

As you deliver your commercial *focus on the camera only.* Do not look at the casting director, producer, or anyone else. These people, no matter how important, are immaterial for the moment. Only the camera is important. Remember, the tape will be sent to New York, and as soon as you look into the camera, you will be speaking to the executives who will be watching you in a screening room there.

You will start your commercial by stating your name and the name of your agency. It is mandatory that you give this information in the *mood* of the commercial you will be reading for. Should you be reading for the role of the efficient secretary, for example, you would state your name and agency in a completely different manner than if you were reading for the part of the young housewife next door. After you have given this information, do not start the commercial immediately, but give your audience about two seconds to get to know your face. It's human nature to want to know with whom one is dealing. Therefore, if you start your commercial right away, the viewers will miss several seconds of the commercial as they look at your face and as such will miss out on absorbing the message of the commercial.

Remember to keep your appropriate energy level until the very end. Do not permit yourself to drop this level. End your commercial by looking at the camera.

THE AUDITION IS OVER

Your interview is *not* over after you have read your last line. As I said, keep up your energy level until the very end. I have seen actors do beautiful readings but, as they finished, they virtually "dropped a curtain," putting an invisible wall between them and the audience. Usually this doesn't affect the final decision on this actor's chances of getting the part, but it does leave a sour note.

Another mistake that actors make is to drag out the audition by

---

*Your script is called *copy* when you read for a commercial.

asking all kinds of questions about interpretation of the role, projected shooting date, length of shooting time, and so on, none of which are concerns of theirs at this moment. The best policy is that after you have read, take a moment to get out of the character, then, as your friendly, likable self, thank the casting director for the opportunity of letting you read, say your good-byes, and leave with your head held high and a smile on your face. Of course you may collapse—you deserve it, you owe it to yourself after the rigors of a reading—but *wait* until the door or the casting director's office has closed behind you.

Immediately after reading you should give your agent a call. If you wish, you may give her some short information about the reading, but refrain from going into a long dissertation about the pros and cons of your audition. At this point your response to your work is highly unreliable.

After several hours, once you have gained some emotional distance, go over your audition mentally. Jot down what you have done well and where you think some improvement is in order, then forget about the audition. Don't make a nervous wreck of yourself trying to decide whether you'll get the part or not. There are only two possibilities: Either you get the part or you don't. If the first alternative is true, you will have fretted about nothing, if the second, no fretting or worrying will get you the part. Right?

Do not feel rejected if you don't get the part. There are so many intangibles involved in a casting decision over which you have no control. Even if you gave a super reading and are perfectly right typewise, you may still lose out.

Following are a few of the most common reasons why actors who are *right* for a part are not chosen:

- *Match.* Let's say you are reading for the part of a father and your son or daughter have already been cast but they could never resemble you in a million years—so you lose out. You might be up for the role of one of four high school friends. Two of the women are blondes; if you are another blonde, you could lose out simply because of the color of your hair. There is a possibility, if they really liked your reading, that they would consider asking you to change your hair color, but most likely they will choose a redhead instead.
- *Age.* You may be just a trifle too young or too old for the part.
- *Height.* You may be too tall or too short for the part in question, or there may be a discrepancy in height between you and your partner.
- *Personality.* You may be too close in personality to another performer already cast.
- *Power and looks.* You may overpower or be better looking than the well-known actor or actress starring in the series or film.

As you can easily see, all of these factors have nothing to do with your talent, personality, or the effectiveness of your reading. True, you may have lost the job, but the reading was still beneficial to you, because you had a chance to demonstrate your talent to the casting director and possibly the director and producer as well. These people will remember you. Believe me, everyone remembers a good actor, because there are not too many outstanding actors around. In ways unknown to you at this moment, more readings will come your way.

If you gave an excellent reading, even if you did not get the part, the audition was successful.

THE ACTOR'S
PUBLIC
RELATIONS

As one speaks about public relations (PR), the mind immediately calls forth pictures of elegant suites of offices in which high-salaried PR people strain their creativity and imaginations to get your beautiful or handsome face onto the front pages of magazines that enjoy nationwide distribution, who make extensive phone calls long-distance to get you on the panel of a popular television talk show, or who coerce gossip columnists and the paparazzi to gather around you as you step out of your chauffeur-driven limousine to attend this or that opening.

True, all of the above *is* PR, but it's PR on the star level, not the PR we are talking about. You will agree that PR is necessary for the stars, but you are just starting out, so why do you need PR? It doesn't matter whether you are just starting out or are an established star, everyone needs PR. The star needs PR to stay on top, whereas the newcomer needs it to become visible, in order to get his or her face and name known in the industry.

The truth is you cannot get started without PR. Naturally it is impossible for the newcomer to pay the eight hundred dollars a month that the PR firm charges for services. So, very simply, you will have to be your own PR person. On a basic level PR is the concept of *making a certain product visible to the public.* Agreed, you are not a product, but your acting ability is a product that has to be sold. Selling this ability is, in principle, the same as if you were, say, selling an antique. If you were to start your own shop, you wouldn't just announce your new business venture to a few friends and neighbors and then sit back waiting for the phone to ring. If you did, your business would fail quickly. No, you would promote your business, you would promote your product. You would make sure that the name of your store and products were known in your town. You would attract clients by displaying your antiques as attractively as possible and maybe exhibit some of them at a fair. You would study the market, checking around for new office openings and inquiring to see whether they might use some of your antiques for display. You would find out what kinds of antiques were in vogue at the present. *You would develop new leads,* contacting interior decorators, restaurants, and hotels. You would visit collectors. And last but not least, *you would stay in contact,* letting all these people know whenever you got a new shipment. At times you might mail out some advertisements to remind them that you are still in business, because staying in contact is the secret of success. All of these actions add up to an *effective sales campaign.*

The same holds true for you the actor. You must promote your product.

- Get your face and name known in the industry
- Study the market
- Stay in contact
- Develop new leads

However, don't expect immediate results. According to a national survey on the promotion of life insurance, the following odds emerge:

- Seventy-five percent of all sales are made after the fourth call on the same prospect
- Twenty-five percent of all salespeople quit after the second call on the same prospect
- Five percent politely but persistently keep calling
- Out of one thousand solicitations by mail, 1 percent (yes, only 1 percent) will result in a sale

Whenever you feel that your PR is just a waste of time and money, look at the foregoing figures and keep on truckin'. In the beginning of your career you must remember that you have to be a terrific mail salesperson.

Don't expect to get an interview after you have mailed your first batch of PR, but keep on mailing and mailing. It is a proven fact that actors who keep up their PR campaigns are the ones who usually win out.

GETTING YOUR FACE
AND NAME KNOWN

The first step in your publicity campaign is to make the industry familiar with your face and name. Remember that our chapter on photography stressed that your headshot look exactly like you? That you should take great care in selecting your headshot, since it will become your trademark for the next two years at least? Your goal at this point is to establish a correlation between your name and your trademark, that is, establish an *image*.

For this reason you should use the same headshot in all your promotional endeavors. Don't confuse the industry by sending or using different headshots, showing different hairdos and moods. This is very important. For example, if you went to the store to buy your favorite brand of coffee that is usually packaged in blue and white but one day it appeared on the shelves in réd, you would have a hard time finding your brand of coffee as you search for the familiar blue and white label. Your image and the coffee labels have been established in the same *specific* way. So, be sure to use the same headshot, which will become your trademark, on all mail-outs to agents, casting directors, thank-you postcards, in the Academy Players Directory, and in all trade advertisements.

Fortunately your mail-outs do not require a great deal of money, but they do require a great deal of *persistence, work, and time.*

At this point it doesn't pay to spend a lot on publicity for the simple reason that there is not yet much to publicize. It is true, that there are some actors who are paying for full-page advertisements in the trade and some who pay huge amounts for renting billboards on Sunset Strip in Hollywood. While one or the other of these actors may see results, generally such extravagant publicity has proven to be a waste of money.

Yes, there is great value in advertising in *Daily Variety* and *The Hollywood Reporter,* once you have *something* to promote. If you get a part, even a tiny one on a TV show, *then* you should advertise, *then* it will pay to advertise. You don't need a full page; an eighth of a page showing your name and trademark picture, information as to what show you will be appearing in, the date and time of the broadcast, as well as your agent's name are all that are needed. A bigger or more expensive ad is particularly unnecessary because your name and face will already have been promoted effectively via the Academy Players Directory. (Remember, you do not have to be a member of a union to be placed in this directory, but you do have to have an agent.) And casting directors have your résumé and headshots as well as your mail-outs, that excellent PR tool that you have faithfully sent out informing them of your progress in the industry. In short, you have handled your PR in a consistent and businesslike manner.

When you are going to appear on a TV show or in a film, you will *definitely* want to mail your picture postcards to the casting directors. You will be surprised at how many will tune in to watch you. If you are appearing on TV, send your cards to *all* casting directors, whether or not you have had an interview with them.

Here is an example of what an effective PR postcard should look like:

Please watch me in:

SHOW   Fantasy Island _____

ROLE   Bartender _____

TIME AND DATE   Thursday, May 5, 8:00 P.M. _____

CHANNEL   9 _____

DEMO TAPES

Probably the most effective tool to promote and show your ability as a screen actor is the demo tape. Unfortunately many actors are misled into spending a large amount of money having a tape made that shows them either in short or, worse, in long monologues, or in a scene performed at a college or community theater. No casting director will look at such tapes.

There are a number of video studios that advertise so-called demonstration tapes that show the actor in a mock commercial. Even though some of these tapes are excellent and of good professional quality, the money spent is usually not consonant with the results achieved. Most casting directors will not view these tapes, and it is unlikely that you will get an interview by sending them out. If you are just starting out, though, you may get an agency who will be willing to look at them. However, the agencies are usually more interested in the actor's personality than they are in the mock commercial. So it would be more to the actor's benefit simply to present himself giving a friendly chat, telling about his background, hopes, and aspirations. With the aid of such an honest, unpretentious tape, agents will be able to evaluate any prospective client.

The only tapes worth your money and effort are those that show you in actual film or TV performances. Short segments of films that are currently in distribution or TV shows and commercials that are on the air are best. These tapes will carry much weight with agents and casting directors alike. Naturally, no actor just beginning will be able to supply such valuable tapes, because the beginning actor usually has no screen credit.

But—remember the chapter on how to find jobs in the film industry? You were advised to participate in college film and TV productions, right? Make certain you get a duplication of your scene made. If the project was video-taped, you can get this done the day of your performance. If the project was filmed, it will take a little longer, depending on how soon the film is edited. Most likely you will have to pay for the film or tape yourself. In any case *you* must supply the college with your own tape, which has to be comparable to the tapes that they use, either ½-inch or ¾-inch size. A ¾-inch tape must serve you better, since mostly ¾-inch machines are used by the industry. There should be no cost for making the "dupe,"* since duplication equipment is usually available at most college tele-communication departments.

An effective demo tape should not be longer than three minutes. It should show, first, some good close-ups of your face. These close-ups should show *vitality and energy* and should highlight your *own personality.* Show yourself off to your best advantage. Also choose some short scenes that show you with other actors. These scenes do not have to have continuity, that is, make sense as a story line.

Most importantly you should select scenes that show your acting ability and your ability to react to a partner. These scenes *must* demonstrate your screen personality.

Agreed, this kind of demo tape can be costly, since it has to be done professionally by a good video editing lab. You will find various listings in the Yellow Pages. Shop around, because their fees vary greatly.

If you have scenes from a professionally produced film, by all means give your screen credits on the tape. Regardless of whether you show your professional film clips or scenes from your grad films, have your name and the name of your agency appear on the tape. Agents and casting offices have to deal with an avalanche of tapes, and tapes can easily get lost. Therefore, make certain that your name and your agent's name, address, and telephone number are listed on the cassette as well.

The best policy is to hand-carry your cassette to the various offices. Don't leave your precious, and very expensive, tape anywhere longer than fourteen days. This time span is sufficient for anyone to view a short tape, no matter how busy he or she may be.

ACTORS' SHOWCASES

It is important for you to participate in as many good stage productions as will comfortably fit in with your schedule, be they college, community, or

---

*Dupe refers to the duplication of a video tape.

Equity-waiver productions. But do not expect to be seen by casting directors and agents. In most cases, these showcases are no showcase for your talent. The purpose of these productions is for you to practice your craft, to get more comfortable in your acting technique. Both New York and Los Angeles have such a selection of excellent Equity-waiver productions,* that casting directors and agents cannot possibly attend all of them.

If you have a substantial part in an Equity-waiver production, one that shows you off to your best advantage, definitely invite the casting directors with whom you have had interviews. You also might wish to invite some agents who are a step or two above the agent who is now representing you. Still, you might get only a few of the people you invited to see the show, unless you are already well known in the industry and your work is recognized.

As mentioned before, there are some acting schools and workshops that showcase their students periodically. Such a showcase might serve you well, since the coach usually knows some agents, directors, and casting directors. However, your best choice is to look for a *professional showcase,* that is to say, a well-known and reputable theater that will present about fifteen three-minute scenes during the lunch hour and invite industry people *free.* The viewing participation of industry personnel is excellent, since these people have the chance to view *many* actors in a comparably short period of time. These showcases are highly beneficial once you have reached the professional level, but do not attempt to participate in such a showcase unless you are sure of your acting ability.

All showcases operating on this basis will audition prospective participants first. You must be an accomplished actor to be accepted and, if chosen, you must pay an established fee. You are completely on your own in these showcases, since the scene you bring in, will *not* be directed by anyone connected with the administration of the showcase.

As you select your scene, keep the following in mind:

- Keep your scene short. Three minutes is plenty of time to show your acting ability.
- Choose a partner who will support but not outshine you.
- Make sure that your audition material has not already been done over and over. Casting directors have seen *Our Town* and *Rainmaker* too much. Do yourself a favor and find something relatively new and unknown.
- Avoid heavy dramatic scenes. Save those for your workshop. Short, upbeat scenes will catch the casting director's attention best.

*An Equity-waiver production is a show being performed in a 99-seat house, and hiring members of AEA (American Equity Association). However, actors performing in such a show do not have to be paid equity rates, as these only appear once a house has 100 seats. At times actors performing in an "equity waiver" will not get paid.

- Select a character that suits your own personality and is within your own age range.
- Get immediately to the point of the scene that calls for the strongest reaction. Find the moment that grabs the viewer's attention *immediately*.
- Avoid any "stretching." Bring in a scene in which you feel comfortable.
- Have fun.

OFFICE SCENES

Many of the network casting offices, such as NBC, CBS, and ABC, cast popular soaps (morning soap operas) and will see *audition scenes* or *office scenes*. To do such a scene is an excellent way of introducing yourself to the casting directors as well as of showing your craft.

You should call the casting office and ask whether or when they hold such auditions. Once you have gotten this information, you should send in your picture and résumé immediately, requesting that you be placed on the list of actors to be seen. Call in every so often and find out when the auditions will be scheduled. About two weeks before the audition date, call back and make sure that your name is still on the list.

You have the best chance of being seen if you are either very young, very good-looking or handsome, or definitely a character actor. The middle range of "leading lady" or "leading man" has less of a chance getting an audition. Casting directors have long backlogs of experienced actors in this particular age range. This doesn't mean that you should be discouraged at the very start or fail to request such an audition. Incidentally, you do not have to be represented by an agent or be a member of either SAG or AFTRA to be seen in an office scene.

PERSISTENCE

In the beginning of your professional acting career very little time will be spent on auditions and interviews. This is the time to develop and promote your career. It is up to you to make your career *happen*. Persistence is very important. You must send out your pictures and postcards again and again. Many of your pictures will end up in the wastebasket, but if only a few get you an interview with an agent or casting director, *if you can get your foot in the door,* it's all worthwhile. There is a tremendous amount of competition in this business, but those who persist, who request interviews, follow up with thank-you notes, keep contacts alive by informing people about their progress, these actors have a better chance of making it than those who only rely solely on their agents. The more contacts you have, the greater your opportunities. Do not leave the job of promoting you up to your agent. It is only *you* who can create the energy and therefore *movement* in your chosen profession.

HOW TO JOIN
THE UNIONS

As an actor, you will be dealing with the following unions:

SAG   Screen Actors Guild

AFTRA   American Federation of Television and Radio Artists

SEG   Screen Extras Guild

AGVA   American Guild of Variety Artists

AEA   Actors Equity Association

In order to be able to work for a signatory film, television show, or commercial, you must be a member of SAG. To get a SAG card is quite an achievement for the new actor. In fact, the SAG card is looked upon as a sign of "knighthood," of belonging to a select, if rather large, group.

Many new actors labor under the impression that they can merely join SAG in order to belong. This is not true. The regulation states that no actor should be permitted to join unless he or she has a SAG job. This means that *if* she is hired by a film, television, or commercial company that is signatory with SAG and as such promises only to hire SAG actors, only then can she get a SAG card. So far so good. However, another regulation states that no actor can accept a SAG job unless he is a member of SAG. Therefore the new actor is faced with a perfect example of "which came first, the chicken or the egg?" You cannot join SAG unless you have a SAG job, and you cannot get a SAG job unless you are a member of SAG.

110

Fortunately in reality things are a little less complicated. Once you have been hired for a SAG signatory film or television show, all that is necessary is to get a letter written by the producer stating the fact of your employment, and *presto,* you will be accepted by SAG. This also holds true for commercials.

The ruling for such acceptance is the following:

- You must have at least *three days'* work on a film or television show.
- You must have at least *one day's* work on a commercial.

Therefore, a one-day job on a film or television show will not get you into SAG. Realistically you will agree that it is almost impossible for the new actor to get into the union via television or feature films. Taking into consideration the fact that half-hour TV shows take five days to shoot and an hour-long television show takes from ten to twelve days, you can see that three days' work represents a sizable part. Furthermore, it is seldom that a new actor is given a sizable role on television. Now you can see why it's not so easy to join SAG via television.

For feature films the picture looks somewhat better. It is true that the number of major studio films that are shot in relation to television is small, but getting a part with a small independent SAG film will bring you your union membership. (If the film is non-union, then no matter how substantial your role, you will *not* get your SAG card.) Fortunately for the beginning actor, the number of small independently produced films is on the increase.

Things look even brighter when we speak about commercials. Here the ruling is that you only have to work for one day in order to join SAG. Furthermore, it is not necessary for you to say lines, but you do have to be a principal in the commercial.

Being new in Hollywood or New York, you may be greatly baffled by the term *Taft-Hartley* when an actor speaks to you about union membership. The Taft-Hartley law is a ruling that permits a non-union person (actor or otherwise) to work *one* union job without joining the union. I would strongly advise against taking advantage of this law, however. In order to get consistent work, one *must* be a member of SAG.

You will also hear other unions mentioned. SEG (Screen Extras Guild) is self-explanatory. AGVA (the American Guild of Variety Artists) encompasses night club acts, night club performers, skaters, and circus performers. AEA (Actors Equity Association) is the union responsible for stage actors. AFTRA (American Federation of Radio and Television Artists) pertains to radio and television, both live and taped; this includes sitcoms, soap operas, and a few game shows. All these shows are technically AFTRA, but SAG as well as AFTRA performers work in these areas, since the line is rather dimly drawn.

For the new actor, AFTRA is important insofar as he or she doesn't have to show an AFTRA job in order to join this union. As a matter of fact, anyone, even without any acting background, is allowed to join AFTRA simply by paying the initiation fee and the required dues. Still, it is beneficial for you the new actor to join AFTRA because you will more easily acquire a SAG card due to this affiliation and thus be channeled into the mainstream of the industry.

The SAG ruling is that *any* member of a *sister union,* such as AFTRA, AGVA, and AEA, can become a member of SAG *one year after* she or he has completed *one job* within the framework of that sister union. The important fact is that while SAG draws a distinction between extras and actors, AFTRA doesn't. Therefore any job you do as an extra on an AFTRA show counts as an AFTRA job and can move you toward your SAG membership. So as soon as you join AFTRA, get on the extra casting lists of the soaps that shoot under AFTRA contracts. You may have to wait several months before you are called in, but eventually you will be doing your AFTRA job. There are quite a few people who have worked their way up this way. They started as extras, then were given parts "under five lines," later bits (which is more than five lines). Some even became "regulars"* on soaps.

Actors as well as producers often complain about the unions, yet there has to be an institution that protects its members and is a place for arbitration. In addition to this basic protection the unions also have health benefits and credit unions. All the guilds operate under a charter of the Labor Congress of Industrial Organizations (AFL/CIO). SAG and AFTRA maintain offices in all of the major cities.

*The term *regular* pertains to an actor who appears consistently on a series or soap.

DON'T EXPECT A HOME RUN RIGHT AWAY

Almost everyone who comes to Hollywood or New York and reaches out for the golden ring of recognition usually has something going for him or her, be it looks, personality, talent, or the rare and beautiful combination of all of these attributes. The sad truth is that almost everyone arriving has been outstanding back home. Confident about themselves and flushed with success, these actors who were so experienced in their high school or college productions, soon have to realize that neither Hollywood nor New York welcomes them with open arms. They must prove themselves all over again.

Eddie Foy, a long-time casting director and an experienced and knowledgeable man, expressed the following opinion: "Actors come to town because someone in their hometown said that they were the best in their community theater production. They come here and expect all doors to be open. The best advice I can give to an actor is to be professional. Know your craft. I like to use actors who have paid their dues, who studied and deserve the opportunity, who are dedicated and true to our business."

Renee Valaente, one of Hollywood's most outstanding casting directors and a person who has many years of experience casting for the major studios, has the following advice: "Don't expect a home run right away. Settle for a single. What is important about success is starting at the bottom. Slowly you get taller and walk straighter. Success means two things: knowledge and the people you know, but first is the knowledge."

"I cannot underestimate the importance of being prepared," states Geoffrey Fisher, who spent many years casting for Universal Pictures. "We

114

are an industry that is very slow to forget a mediocre or poor performance. It is very important for actors to continue to study. Many a talented individual has been in too deep over his head the first time out and has to spend years overcoming it."

Talking to casting directors, producers, and agents, the new actor will get pretty much the same advice. The consensus boils down to this: *Be prepared* and *know your craft.*

You must understand and accept fully that an actor's training is a long, winding road until she reaches a level of craft that permits her even to make a start in the film business.

Let's discuss the various areas of training.

ACTING CLASSES IN COLLEGE

For most budding actors who have enjoyed a measure of success in high school plays and drama clubs, the next logical step is to enroll in drama classes at the local college. In smaller towns the local liberal arts or community college may be the only place to study, because there may be no other good acting school around. College classes provide a helpful proving ground for new actors. It is there that they will learn the basic skills of their craft. The college drama department offers the opportunity to participate in a variety of campus theatrical productions. This experience exposes aspiring actors to the strict discipline of rehearsals. In addition, they learn to adapt to the pressure of performing for an audience that is more demanding than were those of their high school days. Most important, they have the assurance of being taught by knowledgeable and experienced teachers whose credentials and backgrounds have been thoroughly checked.

If the aspiring actor decides to earn his college degree, then he has to attend a number of often demanding classes that are required to fulfill the general education requirements, in addition to his beloved acting classes. It may happen that during the first two years, he will spend less time on acting classes than on demanding academic subjects.

Going the college road means going the long road. Aspiring actors will attend a series of classes that will gradually lead them to the basic knowledge and application of their craft. You must be willing to spend a lot of time and effort to survive in college drama courses, but there is no shortcut as far as acting is concerned. If you attend a community college, you will spend two years, four years at a liberal arts college, toward learning your craft.

So the question is "Should I go into acting right away or should I get a college degree first?" This question has several answers.

First, if you are not living in Los Angeles or New York or any major metropolis that offers good acting opportunities and if you have not done any acting of any consequence, my advice would be to go to college and work toward your degree in Drama for at least two years. However, if you are already based in either Los Angeles or New York and you are thinking seriously about making acting your livelihood, my advice would be different: Don't go to college, but get started working toward your acting career right away. The most opportune age for the beginning actor is from eighteen to twenty-two years old, precisely the years you would spend pursuing your college degree.

Of course, you might try both, attending college and pursuing an acting career at the same time. But the danger exists that one or the other will suffer.

Both Los Angeles and New York offer an abundance of first-class acting workshops and coaches whose names are known industrywide, and in some cases worldwide. If you are a beginning acting student, it is unlikely that any of these coaches will accept you, since they usually refuse any student who doesn't have a solid background in acting. But you do have a wide variety of excellent acting schools to choose from, though you may be hesitant about enrolling in any of them.

If you are unable to find good, reliable acting classes for beginners or intermediates, you should turn toward college. Perhaps you are not interested in studying any academic subjects but wish instead to attend acting classes only. In this case you can scan through the extension series catalog of any college and find various acting classes taught mostly by instructors who are personally active in the field of acting. These courses are very good.

Some schools have a telecommunications department. Try to register with this department immediately upon enrollment so that you can be considered for their film and tape projects. This will give you some good basic training as far as camera acting is concerned. You will not be taught camera technique, but by observing your screen performance you can get an idea of what you do well and where you need improvement. You would also do well to take some diction classes, as well as courses in history, literature, and psychology. These classes will help inform you of various places and different times, opinions, and mores. The psychology class will give you insight into how people "tick."

If you do not live in Los Angeles or New York, DO NOT, and I repeat DO NOT, pack your bags and buy a plane ticket. You will be wasting your time. You will knock on doors without any success. Do not count on taking classes in L.A. or the Big Apple. No, stay put. Stay home for two years and enroll in college; take all your basic classes there, and then try community theater before you spread your wings. The two years at home will come in very handy, because you will gain not only some basic acting knowledge but also some wisdom as far as life is concerned.

It stands to reason that you might not agree with me in my observations, claiming instead that "New York and Los Angeles is where the action is, and even though none of the famous acting coaches will accept you, these cities offer many acting schools where you may study. Agreed, there is an abundance of fine acting schools and dedicated coaches, but you'll also find many mediocre schools that have no business training actors. When you are starting out, you do not have enough experience to be able to judge prospective acting schools and lack knowledge of the basics in the acting craft sufficient to know what kind of school would be right for you. Get at least one year, and hopefully two years, of college acting under your belt before you give the big city a try.

The foregoing advice has been directed primarily to the recent high school graduate, but it applies to mature men and women as well. You are the group of people who fall prey so easily to mediocre acting schools, and this for the very reason that you have some reluctance to attend college classes and compete with "kids." You are the people who shy away from college, reasoning that you are only taking classes for fun and recreation. As a result, you often enroll in acting classes that offer little real acting instruction. If these classes serve their recreational purpose, fine, but many mature students enroll in the hope of fulfilling a long-cherished and often denied aspiration. If you wish to work toward an acting career, save your money and run, because these schools will not prepare you.

Yes, for you, too, enrolling in college extension classes is the answer. Check with your local college extension, evening division. You will find that for these classes the work load is much easier and is geared toward the working and more mature student. There are neither midterm nor final exams and no tests. Homework is completely voluntary. Taking extension classes will at least give you a taste of what acting is all about. These classes will give you the background that you need in order to judge any acting class in which you may later want to enroll.

FINDING THE ACTING SCHOOL THAT'S RIGHT FOR YOU

Unfortunately, anyone who so desires, can rent office space, get a license, and open an acting school. No proof of expertise is required. Among the many fine schools, which do their utmost to give their students solid instruction, there are a few that care more about the tuition money that the students bring than the instruction they give.

After having attended acting classes in college and acquired some basic knowledge of acting, you must go on to professional acting classes at a professional acting school. As you look for a professional acting school, take some time to shop around. Look at a number of schools before you decide to sign up for classes. Keep in mind that the look of the school is immaterial in comparison to the quality of the instruction. Don't be blinded by beautiful offices, walls adorned with autographed pictures of stars, or long lists of television shows and films in which students of the school have supposedly appeared. Such credits may easily be for work as extras, nothing more.

If you find a school that seems attractive to you, ask to be permitted to watch one class. Any acting teacher worth the name will gladly let you audit.

As you audit, think about whether the class is within your level of experience. Assuming you already have some semesters of college acting classes to your credit, a rank beginner's or amateur class will be a waste of money. If the class is mostly composed of *working* actors who are concerned about polishing their craft, on the other hand, you will be out of your range, and again your money would be wasted. The coach, no matter how willing and able, cannot devote a lot of time to your particular problems, since these are of no interest to the other members of the workshop.

Once you have found a class that is right for your *present level,* watch for the following favorable signs:

- Is the instructor's criticism simple, clear, and to the point?
- Does the instructor criticize and correct *specific* things about the student's performance?
- Does the instructor advise the student to work on these specific things in order to improve his or her technique and/or performance?
- Is the instructor aware of the individual problems of the various students?
- Does the instructor have the class under control?
- Is the atmosphere in the class positive and happy?

Some of the unfavorable signs would be the following:

- Is the critique given by the instructor vague, moving only within the framework of her or his own esoteric opinions?
- Is the critique addressed to many problems at once, confusing the student?
- Is the critique delivered from the floor, allowing all the other students to voice their opinions while the poor actor faces an inquisition?
- Does the instructor like to talk, wasting time as he or she indulges in anecdotes about the movie business, or whatever?

Another equally important fact to consider as you choose an acting school is the instructor's personality. Is it compatible with yours? Are you able to relate to her or him? Do you like and respect the instructor as a person? Do you feel comfortable with him? Can and will you take constructive criticism from him?

If you do not have confidence about the instructor or sense good feelings between you, then you should not join the class. You would be questioning each and every one of her suggestions and critiques.

Last but not least, consider your instructor's credentials. At this point in your career you are *not* looking for the M.A. or Ph.D. behind your instructor's name; you are looking for his *industry affiliations*. Find out if he is *actively* involved as an actor or a director in the film or television business. Trends in acting techniques change subtly over the years, so be sure he is involved *at present*.

Acting schools no longer have a mandatory audition for an actor to be able to join the class. The instructor can get a fairly good impression about an actor's personality, his possible liabilities and assets, via a short informal chat. Genuine acting ability won't surface until after the student has been with the instructor for about a month, so don't take it as "money grubbing" if the instructor suggests that you take her class for a month on a trial basis. Believe me, the instructor knows her business.

Let's assume that you've found the acting school you feel comfortable in and that you work hard learning the specific acting technique taught there. You should nonetheless continue to do student films and should also branch out by auditioning for community theater and Equity-waiver shows. You will only get small parts, since the competition with working actors is great. Yet, every small experience counts, and each part will make you more and more confident.

My suggestion is that you stay *no* longer than six months with any given coach or instructor. By then you will have absorbed what he or she has to offer. After that period of time it will no longer pay to stay, because the work will become repetitious, and you might become a carbon copy of the teacher and his techniques. You should expose yourself to a wide variety of acting coaches and acting styles. You the actor should *pick your technique* from the wide variety you have experienced. As soon as an instructor points you out as a shining example of her technique, it is time for you to leave.

FILM SCHOOL

By now you have a solid stage technique. You know how to dissect a script or play; you know how to portray a character and have gained some experience in fusing the character you portray with your own personality. You have taken a big step toward your final goal, becoming a *film actor*.

The time has come for you to enroll in a good film school. The search for a film school will now be much easier than the search for an acting school was, since you can apply the same criteria. Still, there are a few additional points you should consider.

Pay attention to the composition of class members. Film acting schools unfortunately attract many amateurs. These people are drawn by what they think will be easy money for commercials. Or they are looking for fun and glamor and think that doing a bit part here or there might be exciting. Usually these people don't have the solid acting background an actor should have before attempting a film school. If you do find many amateurs at a school, you had better move on to a different one, since this one is not for actors who are seriously pursuing their acting careers.

Is the video equipment for class use in good condition or is a lot of class time spent on repairs and adjustments?

Is enough time allowed for camera performance, playback, critiques by instructor, and repeat performances by students?

Is the critique clear and does it cover the technical aspects of the actor's performance, such as the use of face and emotion in close-ups, medium shots, and long shots, and the special problems of two-shots.* Be aware that in a good film acting school, basic acting techniques are taken for granted and the instructor will be more concerned with the effectiveness of the actor's performance on screen than anything else.

Does the instructor deal thoroughly with the aspect of individual personality as it comes across on the screen? Watch for the following:

- Have the students been cast properly?
- Are students trained to let their own personality shine and do they effectively fuse this personality with the character they are portraying?

When you judge a film class according to the last-mentioned criterion, you must of course realize that it is basically *your,* not the instructor's, responsibility to develop your most effective personality to the fullest. It is the instructor's job to give you necessary technical tools so that you can *come across on the screen.*

Many actors do not feel the need to attend film acting classes, citing the lack of artistic creativity of the courses. This is true, but the technical aspects of film acting need to be stressed, because actors must have

---

*A *close-up* is a full-face shot, a *medium shot* is to the waist, and a *long shot* is the entire body. A *two-shot* is two people in one shot.

this experience. Casting directors get worried if they see neither film experience nor attendance in a film acting school on your résumé.

The need for learning to work in front of a camera goes deeper. Your stage experience is valuable for your training, but it doesn't necessarily work for film. There are great stage actors who just don't quite make it in film, and of course vice versa. As a screen actor you have to *project your own personality, reaching out of the screen in order to affect your audience.* The audience should not be able to take their eyes off of you. This quality has nothing to do with good looks. It is that certain magnetic quality in the actor's eyes, voice, or his or her entire being that keeps the audience captivated. This must be *you,* not a copy of some star you admire. Besides learning the technical aspects of your craft as far as film acting is concerned, film school is the place where you will work on the effective projection of your screen personality.

Some actors contend that since film is "personality business," they do not need stage acting background. Most knowledgeable people in the film industry disagree. You *do* need a solid stage acting background to survive in this industry, and no matter how you look at it, the stage is the first place you will spread your wings. It is also the place you should always return to for nourishment, regardless of how high or how far you go as a screen actor.

COMMERCIAL WORKSHOPS

Right after you have completed film school, you should attend a commercial class. There are many reputable commercial schools in Los Angeles, New York, and other major cities. Some of these schools are run by casting directors. It is not a bad idea to join one of these, since you will get instruction "from the horse's mouth." Don't join only in the hope that you will be cast by your instructor. Such workshops have many, many students and only a limited amount of jobs, and most of these would go to the more experienced actors anyway.

Remember that the commercial school is interested in your acting only insofar as commercials are concerned, so don't expect any tips on film acting. In selecting a commercial school, you should look for the following:

- Does the instructor stress *immediacy,* that *right-away power* that is so important for commercials?
- Is dialogue handled in an easy, conversational manner?
- Are the actors taught to handle products effectively?

You should base the selection of a commercial school solely on the soundness of the instruction. Don't let your opinion be swayed by the so-called demo tapes and "mock" commercials that some of the schools may offer you. These tapes are usually not worth the money or your time. Don't be swayed also by a school that promises work in commercials. A school is no agency and in reality cannot do this for you. The only thing a school can do for you is to instruct you effectively in one of the various fields of the profession, and believe me, that is a great undertaking in itself.

ACTING WORKSHOPS

There is always a need for actors to study in order to practice their craft and develop aspects of their personalities. They must also learn to deal with performance problems. In short, an actor's learning process never stops. Just because an actor has gotten some bits, some commercials, and has done Equity-waiver or dinner theater shows and possibly some summer stock is no reason for him or her to stop the learning process.

Once you feel secure in your craft, you should join a good workshop, preferably one that would look impressive on your résumé, which means one that is run by a famous coach. Such a workshop could be expensive, but even if you can't afford to study with a name, there are many excellent workshops around.

First, let's discuss *what a workshop is not*. It does *not teach acting*. The prototypes of the world-famous workshop are Actors Studio in New York and Actors Studio West in Hollywood. On the list of their life members you'll find such names as Paul Newman, Marlon Brando, and Maureen Stapleton, just to name a few. The Actors Studio is literally a who's who of famous actors.

Some acting schools call themselves workshops, of course, but when you have reached workshop level, you won't have any trouble distinguishing between an acting class and a workshop.

Also, a workshop is *not a showcase*. Don't expect to be discovered in a workshop. Some good workshops do showcase their members periodically in scenes rehearsed in the workshop and usually directed by the coach, but the true showcase is a cat of a different breed.

So, if the workshop does not teach acting what does it do? It is simply the place where actors can develop their craft and deal with specific creative problems. For this reason you should select a workshop that is guided by a sensitive coach who is blessed with patience and understanding.

A good professional actor's coach is a person who possesses superior acting ability, extensive professional experience, but who also has keen insight into human behavior. Since most roles are combinations woven of overt and subconscious behavior, the coach must understand the emotional makeup of humanity. Yet, a workshop in no way takes the place of psychotherapy, so don't put your coach in the position of leading you step by step through the highways and byways of your own complex personality. Your coach is not a psychoanalyst and the suggestions he or she offers pertain to your personality only insofar as your acting is concerned.

As you choose a workshop, look for the following:

- Do you like and trust the coach?
- Are most of the members of the workshop compatible with you and with each other?
- Will you be able to accept constructive criticism from this group? (This is the place where professional actors give their professional evaluations.)
- Are the other members of the workshop a little above your level in experience and professional ease? (If this is the case, you will learn a lot by observing their performances.)

Some workshops offer valuable and exciting *cold-reading classes.* You should take advantage of this opportunity, since a good cold-reading class is a *must* for every actor. If your workshop doesn't offer this, you should make every effort to find a class of this kind.

A LOOK INTO
THE CRYSTAL BALL

10

Everyone, regardless of his or her chosen profession wants to be a *success*. Whether one is a sales clerk, lawyer, doctor, or teacher, everyone wants and needs success. We actors are not the only ones craving recognition, applause, and money for our efforts. Therefore, write this on the mirror of your bathroom:

> It's okay to want success.
> It's okay to want money.
> It's okay to want applause.
> It's okay to win.
> I am okay.

First, let's clarify what success is in our own minds. It is a fallacy to think of success as stardom. Stardom is a complicated matrix of politics, publicity, and management. The star is only a rather small particle in an enormous machinery. Therefore, let us think of success as a *measure of achievement and reward* in a profession that one enjoys.

Besides politics, acting is probably one of the most difficult professions in which to achieve any measure of success. Struggling for recognition is frustrating. With acting, the most frustrating part is that no matter how skilled an actor, no matter how talented or creative, no matter how much she or he studies or how much effort she puts into promoting herself, she still might not achieve success. In almost any other line of work, one is assured of at least a certain measure of success in proportion to the effort one puts into one' work. Not so with acting.

You are in a profession that knows no regular pay and advancement, where one acting job well done doesn't necessarily lead to a better one, and where many even very good actors are chasing a few available jobs. In short, as an actor you might very likely face a life of insecurity.

THE HIGH-SECURITY PROFILE

Richard Hoyt, Ph.D., a former actor and now psychologist, conducted some highly interesting research regarding the actor's security profile. He states the following:

> During the research, certain commonalities were detected among those actors who rated high on self-esteem which seemed to allow them a greater feeling of security. We will describe the profile first, which you may or may not match. It helps if you are young, tall, come from a primarily urban background and *consider* yourself handsome, good looking or beautiful. The fact that you may not fit into this profile need not prevent you from feeling secure. The research detected many actors who were secure yet didn't fit into the statistical generalities at all. The first thing the high esteem group had in common was the way in which they *identified themselves.* They all thought of themselves as *leads.* It didn't matter what they looked like or what their age was, they all felt O.K. about *who they were.* Their feelings about themselves were reflected in a higher measure of self-esteem and consequently their attitude about the acting profession was different. *They approached it more as a business.* *

Keeping the foregoing statement in mind, let's dissect the high-security profile into its various components in order to find out *how* and in *what* way these affect the actor's attitude toward success.

Talking to agents, one arrives at the following attributes an actor should possess in order to succeed. An agent is more likely to represent you if you have

- Personality
- Looks (handsome and beautiful or possess definite commercial identity)

*Richard Hoyt, Ph.D., and Judith Shevren, Ph.D., "Everything You Always Wanted to Know About Feeling Secure and Confident," *Screen Actor Magazine,* January 1979, p. 8. Copyright Screen Actors Guild, Inc. 1979.

- Youth
- Craft
- Persistence and self-discipline
- Talent

If you are blessed with all of these qualities, you are more likely to succeed than someone who is missing one or two. After having established the *basic criteria* for the most likely candidate for success, let's break these components down and examine their integral values.

Personality

Personality is topmost on the list. Personality is the intangible "something," the *presence* and the *magnetism* that draw others to you, that make the audience want to watch you as you appear on the screen and, most important, make them want to see you again. *Personality is not a talent.* There are many actors who have screen personality and screen presence but only limited talent. Looking at the opposite side of the coin, we find many talented actors in workshops who unfortunately, no matter how excellently they perform, are lacking personality and presence. Others, fully recognizing the importance of personality, pattern themselves after the stars in looks and personality and stress attributes they as individuals do not possess and may even be in direct opposition to their own selves.

True personality and screen presence can only emerge from the subterranean recess of your own soul and individuality.

Looks

Yes, looks are important. It helps if you are handsome or beautiful. We do worship beauty, but paradoxically in Los Angeles and New York beauties are a dime a dozen. Even if you won your local beauty contest or were the most handsome guy in your hometown, *beauty alone will get you nowhere.* True, you might be seen by some agents and consequently get a commercial or two, but your career will be sporadic and short-lived if you do not have other qualities to back it up. There are so many beautiful people around, but if your beauty is strengthened by your *craft* of good solid training, your chances will be much better. And if next to beauty and craft you possess personality, your chances will be very good indeed. Yet, there is more to it.

Remember the old saying "Beauty is only skin deep"? Well, as far as the acting profession is concerned, it might be changed to "Beauty is more than skin deep." *You must feel beautiful in order to look beautiful.* There are many beautiful women and handsome men who seldom exude the aura of beauty, because they do not *think* of themselves as outstanding.

Even if you are not a ravishing beauty, you should learn to make the very most of the assets that you do possess. Do you have either a well-proportioned figure or an enchanting smile? What about your impressive eyes, great legs, or your terrific hair? If you have only one of these attributes and maybe the rest of you is not so great, make the most of it, stress it, let it shine.

If you have any liability that bothers you, by all means try to change it if you can. Changing your looks for the better is not vanity, but very often a psychological necessity, since as soon as you feel more secure about your looks, you feel better about yourself, and consequently you will relate to others in a more positive and effective way. Once you have saved money, it is no great problem in these days of plastic surgery to have your nose shortened, your face tightened, or your skin smoothed. If you feel you are too heavy, go on a diet, exercise, and slim down. Of course, if you are too short or tall, you cannot change that. Be grateful with whatever height or bone structure nature has bestowed upon you and modify it by enhancing your best feature while drawing attention away from the less outstanding ones by using clothes cleverly.

When we speak about looks, we naturally think about beauty, but as far as the acting profession goes, looks don't mean beauty entirely. There are many actors whom one wouldn't call beautiful or handsome (Charles Bronson, Maureen Stapleton, and Clint Eastwood, to name a few), but these actors' looks are so very engaging because their personalities match and correlate so perfectly with the public image they project. So, if you do not fall into the category of handsome or beautiful, don't hand in your SAG card, don't despair, but quickly search for the right look that will strengthen and enhance your personality. Discover the assets in your particular and individual look, those that strengthen and interpret the personality you want to project. Look for those liabilities that may keep you from projecting a public image or personality successfully. Strengthen your assets and reduce your liabilities.

Youth

It is true that the younger you are when you start your acting career, the better your chances. The best age to start is eighteen. We are a youth-oriented society, and the buying audience for the theater is comparatively young. More and more, films, television, and commercials are geared for the young audience.

If you are in your middle years or a senior citizen, your chances of making it are not nearly so good. You will have to work twice as hard as your younger counterpart, and you also have to realize that there are fewer roles available for you. As far as craft is concerned, you have to be a *superior actor* to get your proverbial foot in the door.

Craft

Craft, that is to say, being a well-trained and skilled actor, is the *most important* single factor in determining whether you will succeed or fail. Craft includes not only stage, film, and commercial training but also those workshops, showcases, and grad and thesis films that you participate in after all your basic acting training has been completed. Believe me, *an actor's training never stops.*

Persistence and Self-Discipline

Let's assume you have all the qualities that predestine you to be a success. You are young, beautiful, have a sparkling personality and are a skilled actor. You will still be reaching for the golden ring of success in vain if persistence and self-discipline are missing in your emotional makeup. Acting is such an overcrowded profession that it is difficult to get your foot in the door without persistence, and once you've gotten a foothold, you won't survive without discipline.

For this very reason you cannot go into an acting career unprepared. You cannot pursue an acting career halfheartedly. You must practice your craft and promote yourself *all the time,* not just whenever the spirit moves you. You've got to stay in top physical and mental condition and not permit yourself to "take it easy" or "let things go for a while." Things such as health or good looks have a tendency to go rapidly down the drain if you let yourself deteriorate. All of this takes persistence and self-discipline.

Many actors' only road to success of some measure is persistence and self-discipline, especially those who have neither great personality nor outstanding beauty and only passable acting ability. There are many such run-of-the-mill actors around, who get small parts here and there but do so consistently. They are not blessed with any sudden burst of fame, but they do stay working in the business for many years because agents and casting directors alike recognize them as capable, punctual professionals who know what they are doing. These actors stay working while many others who enjoyed a short period of success, with possibly some fame and money, have been forgotten.

If someone were to ask me to place a bet on three actors, one young and attractive, one possessing personality and talent, and the third blessed with commercial identity as well as persistence and self-discipline, I would always put my money on the third one.

Talent

You might be surprised to see talent placed last on the list. This is a contradiction, because without at least some sprinkling of talent you would never have thought of becoming an actor. However, as a component of success, talent is not nearly as important as one might wish it to be.

What is talent? Talent is not the desire to become an actor, artist, musician, or ballet dancer. Unfortunately many people confuse their desire for a certain art form as talent. Talent is more difficult to define; because of its intangible, elusive nature it is truly mysterious to the mind. Talent is *the ability to do something easily and naturally,* but it is also the joy of doing that which is present whenever you may practice your craft, be it on the stage, film set, or in a workshop. Talent is a feeling within and about you that comes through your skin and your body and transmits itself to your audience.

Unfortunately, as far as success is concerned, even the greatest talent rarely succeeds without persistence and self-discipline.

Luck

Luck plays an important part in success, there's no doubt about it. A career cannot be made without luck. Still, it is actors themselves who have the responsibility of helping Lady Luck along. It is you actors who have to keep the ball rolling. It is you who are often behind the lucky breaks you get. Maybe a year ago you gave a great cold reading and kept the contact alive by sending out postcards. Maybe you had impressed a director or casting director in a showcase, or possibly your coach may have recommended your work and dedication to some friend who has another friend who needs your particular type for a movie she is casting. No matter how far from left field an actor's lucky break may come, in the last analysis his work and craft are behind them all.

Getting that lucky break is not enough if you do not, as they say, deliver. If your craft, your ability to perform and function under stress, fails you, you might lose out. This is why some children of well-known actors, who are blessed with all the built-in lucky breaks, sometimes don't make it. Luck goes even deeper than making one's own breaks. Luck or the lack of it, is, in the last analysis, self-induced success or failure.

And this in turn is determined by your attitude about yourself and others. You might be the most dedicated, persistent, and self-disciplined actor and still not get ahead. The doors seem closed. You work harder, get more intent upon success, and yet all you encounter is failure. The payoff for all your hard work and effort is frustration. The dedicated and disciplined and continually frustrated actor is a special phenomenon of the acting profession. Dedication that results in frustration is a condition that affects many actors, and it is a condition that leads away from success to failure. Let's discuss this profile in depth.

THE FAILURE PROFILE

Remember high school? Remember Pavlov's dog, that cute little critter? Remember how he was trained? Whenever a bell rang, a bowl of food was set before him. Finally the pooch began to salivate at the sound of the bell whenever it rang, whether food was served or not. The dog had begun to associate the sound of the bell with food. He responded to a signal.

Overreacting to Signals

We do the same, we all respond to signals. Our brain acts like a computer. Memories of past experiences become stored information upon which we draw as soon as we encounter the same or similar situations. These positive or negative connotations call forth our positive or negative responses.

Sir Charles Sherrington, an expert in the field of brain physiology, contends that in the process of learning, a pattern of neurons, similar to a pattern recorded on tape, is set up in our brain. These patterns are replayed whenever we remember past experiences. Dr. Maxwell Maltz, in his book *Psycho-Cybernetics,* goes somewhat further, stating,

> Science confirms a *tattooing* pattern in your brain. When you re-activate patterns out of the past, you re-activate the feeling tone that accompanies them. If we are habitually frustrated by failure, we are apt to acquire habitual feelings of failure which color all our undertakings. On the other hand, if a success pattern can be established, then we activate the feeling of "winning."*

Taking the above statements for granted, we must conclude that we are not reacting to signals as they are, but to signals as we perceive them. Due to the particular taping or tattooing, we react in a computerized or habitual way.

*Maxwell Maltz, M.D., *Psycho-Cybernetics* (Englewood Cliffs, N.J.: Prentice-Hall, Inc., 1960). p. 23. © 1960 by Prentice-Hall, Inc.

Take, for instance, the signal for a "family reunion." It usually calls forth a positive response, since most of us tend to correlate such an event with warmth, love, and fun at the prospect of seeing relatives and old friends whom we haven't seen for some time. It makes us happy to think of exchanging information and feeling that we are home again. Still, there are many of us to whom this signal may call forth a negative response, an immediate reaction of avoidance, since we associate family reunions with cranky old uncles and aunts whom we hardly remember and with being subjected to our cousin's inquiries about our life-style. We tire thinking of listening to our sister's repetitive complaints about the sad state of her marriage. If such negative associations persist for some time, then even *after these situations have changed,* our first response to the signal of "family reunion" will be negative. Even if the cranky old uncle has moved to Florida, the inquisitive cousin is not attending, and our sister is safely tucked away in Reno awaiting her divorce, no matter. The stored information tells us to react to a negative signal. The reaction is habitual.

We are all creatures of habit. Habitually we patronize a familiar grocery store even though the one closer is cheaper. Habitually we reach for the same brand of coffee or cereal. In short, we feel secure in surroundings or situations we are familiar with, whether these situations are positive or not. The crucial point is our familiarity with them. The implication is that we are *taped* to feel secure in either success or failure.

These failure or success signals may have been established in our "computer" in earliest childhood, and they may easily be the reason why some people succeed and others fail.

The sad truth is that no one wants failure, yet some of the most talented, beautiful actors who crave success and work hard toward achieving it *fail.* Unknown to them, they feel secure in failure. In other words, they are taped or tattooed for failure because it is a territory they are familiar with, whereas subconsciously success is viewed as an alien and therefore a threatening experience.

Take a good look at the most common failure profiles. If you are one of those hardworking, deserving actors who is always chasing after success, always hoping to find that it's just around the corner, you might fit into one of these profiles.

The Poor-Little-Me Syndrome

"Poor Little Me" is probably the person most comfortable in failure. Poor little me wraps failure around himself like a warm coat, protecting himself from the harsh winds of reality and the responsibility of achievement. He is used to failure and knows how to handle it and unknowingly gets his reward from failure. He sees himself as the victim of either people or circumstances and doesn't realize that it is he who *permits* others to victimize him. He doesn't realize that it is his reactions that often turn situations against him. Poor little me works very hard and goes a long way to make sure he will fail. Why?

Poor little me has been *rewarded* for failure. The odds are, that one of his parents has always helped him a great deal by doing his homework or writing his papers for him. He was cuddled and spoiled when ill ("Poor little Johnny is so delicate"). He was probably rewarded for poor grades in math because "the teacher was too demanding." He was given cookies and ice cream for his pain when the neighborhood bully kicked him in the shin, and on and on. *Poor little Johnny was always rewarded if someone or something got the better of him. He was always rewarded for failure, but he was never rewarded for success.* Since Johnny now subconsciously expects failure and accepts it as a way of life, he looks for some authority figure to take the place of the rewarding parent. Acting and all the people connected with it, such as coaches, agents, casting directors, take the place of the rewarding parent. Since poor little me has always been rewarded for failure, he now in some mysterious way *expects* to be rewarded for it in his acting career. Responding to his established tapes, in short, he avoids success.

The poor-little-me syndrome is particularly unfortunate to observe in those hardworking professional actors who appear in showcase after showcase and are constantly searching for a new agent. Many of them are talented, have good looks, creative ability, and acting skill, but they continually blow their chances. They tell the world, "Look at me, how hard I work, and still nothing ever happens." Sitting in the wings, they bemoan their fate.

If you should find something of yourself in poor little me, please realize that no one in the adult world is going to reward your for your failure, so you'd better start getting your rewards from success.

The Cinderella Syndrome

Cinderella is a highly refined, very fragile, and unfortunately very common version of poor little me.

A true Cinderella (male or female) works hard but seldom puts out the same effort as poor little me. Such diligent work is not necessary for her, because, after all, Cinderella will be discovered. Right? You can spot a true Cinderella as easily as you can a polka-dotted tiger. A Cinderella happily accepts each and every extra part that comes along. To her, she is not doing extra work for money or to gain some experience, far from that. Cinderella happily slushes through the mud along with the rest of the cast of thousands, knowing in her heart it will be she who is discovered to "carry the spear." When selecting a workshop or coach, Cinderella is not nearly so interested in the quality of instruction as she is in whether or not the coach has the "right connections." She selects her friends on the basis of whether or not they "know the right people." In short, a true Cinderella will grace the coffee counter at Schwab's Drugstore in Hollywood hoping to be discovered, even on the Last Day of Judgment.

Cinderellas are probably the most naive and unrealistic of all actors, and unfortunately the most childlike. If you suspect that some Cinderella has sneaked into your emotional makeup, please realize that life is *not* fair. Life doesn't bestow presents upon you like a fairy godmother. You are behind each and every lucky break you get.

The Guilty-Party Syndrome

The guilty-party syndrome is probably the most serious of all the syndromes mentioned. Some actors who fall into this category work so terribly hard that they might even be termed workaholics. Often they shouldn't be in this business at all, because acting works as a punishment device for them. They might go to great lengths to make certain they will be rewarded only infrequently for their efforts. Most of those who fall into this category are lacking either personality, talent, or commercial identity, which makes it difficult for anyone to make a living as an actor. Still, they persist in their careers.

These actors usually grew up in a family environment in which success was stressed but not sufficiently rewarded. They may also have come from backgrounds in which success was desired but rarely achieved. These actors want success and work very intelligently and diligently toward achieving it, but subconsciously treat it as something to be avoided.

When we talk to actors in this category, we usually discover that their parents were authoritarian, strict, and often hypocritical. The indulgence that often took place in poor little me's background seldom took place as far as "guilty party" was concerned. This is also the reason why it is so difficult to peg actors as members of the guilty-party group. They never complain the way poor little me does. They never rely on others the way Cinderella does. They quietly keep a stiff upper lip as they work toward success, which of course in the scheme of things usually eludes them. Each and every failure strengthens their determination to go on and on and on. For the most part, they are pretty competent actors, but as soon as success beckons, they will fail, for one reason or another.

If you feel you fall into this category, ask yourself the following:

- Do I set my goals too high for the present moment?
- Do I make sure I am not ready right now to join a certain workshop, look for a bigger agency, be seen in a showcase, or audition for casting directors because I still have months of studying ahead of me?
- Do I overload my day with so much busywork that I make sure it cannot all be accomplished and find I am always running after myself?

COMPONENTS OF THE FAILURE PROFILE

Let's face it; all of us during our darker moments fall into one or the other or all of these categories. Moments of self-defeat, unrealistic expectations, and feeling sorry for ourselves occur now and then. We all have times of fear when we'd rather fail than put ourselves and our abilities on the line. This is natural and has to be expected. You will only fall into the failure profile if you display the discussed syndromes in a *continuous* and *predictable* way. It is fairly easy to tell whether you may belong to one of the basic categories.

How to spot a poor little me: He gets his satisfaction as soon as *others feel sorry for him.*

How to spot a Cinderella: She always *depends on others for help.*

How to spot a guilty party: He always *bites off more than he can chew,* making certain he *will not achieve* his goal.

If you break the failure profile down into its most common emotional components, you will find frustration and inhibition at its core.

Frustration

Frustration occurs whenever we fail to achieve a set goal. Achieving just some of our set goals is everyday life. We must understand that a certain amount of failure is normal and therefore chalk it off to experience. A certain amount of frustration is also normal and a part of all our lives. But frustration should not become a *chronic* condition. If we find ourselves in a chronically depressed or frustrated state of mind, we'd better find out if we have set the right goals and if these goals are realistic, or are they simply a device to punish ourselves and as such to perpetuate our frustration.

Inhibition

Inhibition sets in if you have been hurt once too often. Inhibition is a paralyzing emotion that slowly but surely will drain you of self-esteem and the will to succeed. Continuous inhibition may lead to depression. The inhibited person overreacts to the demands of others and represses her or his own feelings. As such, the inhibited person is overly concerned about the opinions of others. Since she reacts mainly to their signals, she permits others to control her. In the last analysis she turns over her life to others, diminishing her own capabilities and potential for success.

In this respect, inhibition is the fear of standing up for one's own rights. It is the fear of being *visible* and, as such, *vulnerable*. Dr. Maxwell Maltz makes the following statement: "The inhibited person's basic frustration is the failure to be himself and to adequately express himself. Frustration is characteristic of practically every area and activity of the inhibited person."*

If you are not quite certain whether you fit into any of the failure profile categories, ask yourself the following questions:

- Do I easily fly off the handle?
- Do I have difficulty falling asleep?
- Do I feel that others are out to get me or that others have all the breaks?
- Do I overload my day with too much to get done so that I seldom accomplish my goals?
- Do I work so hard that I seldom find time for loved ones, friends, or recreation?

The sad fact is that failure can become an emotional habit, a crutch that permits the failure-prone personality to see himself or herself as a *victim*. With such a self-image, failure becomes self-perpetuating.

Considering all of the components of the failure profile, one dominant factor emerges: The failure-prone personality seems to be an individual who takes his cues from another individual rather than initiating action himself. His personality *reacts* rather than *acts*. He waits for another person's signal, to which he will *react* according to long-established "tape" or "tattoo" patterns. Unfortunately his reactions to given signals are most likely to be negative in nature. As he turns his fate over to others, he is like a small child depending on adults.

*Maxwell Maltz, M.D., *Psycho-Cybernetics* (Englewood Cliffs, N.J.: Prentice-Hall, Inc., 1960), p. 78. © 1960 by Prentice-Hall, Inc.

Many people emotionally never reach the adult stage of their lives. They never reach the stage where they create action and are fully responsible for their own lives. Many of us remain children emotionally, adjusting our lives to the demands made by the adults in our environment. It is easy to see that success can only occur if it is based on adult emotions and considerations.

Actors, because of the insecurity of their profession, often feel like children who are being controlled by adults. The adults in the actor's life may be the agent, the casting director, or even the Industry itself. So, if after some soul-searching, you feel that your progress has been stalled by some inherent failure-prone personality traits, and if you decide wholeheartedly to get off this self-defeating and destructive merry-go-round, give some thought to the following:

- Find out the reason why you are failure prone and which of the three given categories you fit into most easily.
- Recognize the *signals* that make you react in a negative way and discard them.
- Work on a *positive* and *realistic* image of yourself and your goals.

THE SUCCESS PROFILE

Dr. Charles Garfield, assistant clinical professor at San Francisco School of Medicine and Nursing, lectures extensively on occupational stress and optimal performance. He makes some interesting observations and bases his contentions on research studies done in past years in Russia and some eastern European countries. He suggests that the people who succeed are those who have learned to tap their *mental capacities*. They are neither specimens for the human potential movement, nor are they trying harder than anyone else.

Faith in themselves and courage in working toward their goal seem to be the main ingredient in their success. Let's take a good look at the success profile.

Faith in One's Own Abilities

Successful people have faith in themselves, and they *never permit anyone to think of them as failures*. No matter how frustrating life may be or how many failures they encounter, they always have the glint of success in their eyes. Even if their successes are small or insignificant, they are proud of their achievements and themselves.

In turn, their self-confidence and knowledge that they are the masters of their own fate lead them to a *happy state of mind.* They accept inner and outer disturbances, frustrations, and failures as par for the course. They seldom overreact to a negative situation and wait cheerfully for a more favorable time to pursue their goals. Therefore, if a situation is difficult or even hopeless, they *do not make it worse* by adding self-pity or resentment. Faith lets them believe that sooner or later the tide will change, and even while waiting, they act on their own behalf, knowing full well that it is up to them to seek success.

Having faith in themselves and their endeavors gives them the strength to live every day of their lives to the fullest. Most are aware that true success comes in small doses and that it must be worked for step by step. They realize that success is not a gift that descends upon the unsuspecting from heaven above, and knowing this, they enjoy each little success, each little joy that the day brings, and try to make the most of every hour of every day. They live in the "now" and are happy right now rather than living on some deferment plan, thinking "I will be happy if I get this part or this TV show." They are happy *while working toward their goals.*

Courage

True courage is in no way the much-proclaimed "quick jump into the cold water." If you subscribe to this theory, you may at times, find yourself in the fire instead of the water. Successful people have learned that it takes courage to make the right decisions at the right time, and as such they take a calculated risk, but not a haphazard one. Decision making for successful people is not a vague weighing of pros and cons but a thoroughly thought-out process. They totally disregard any negative emotional connotations in a given situation because they know that emotions are unreliable as far as decision making is concerned. The first step they take is to acquaint themselves thoroughly with the situation at hand; then they clarify the situation by reducing the problems they are faced with to one sentence only.

Here are some hints you may find helpful in making decisions:

- Gather as much information about the problem as possible. Try to keep from making any decision at this time, because in many cases failure is based on improper information. The failure-prone person usually goes with his or her perceptions and assumptions rather than the facts presenting themselves.
- Consider every alternative. Think about all possible solutions and list them in order. Give them plus and minus points.
- Find out what not to do.

- Pick the solution with the most plus and least minus points and be aware that no solution carries plus points only.

Once a decision is reached and a course of action has been planned, go quickly ahead. Successful people have the *courage* to *act* upon their decisions. They do not wait for them to happen and realize also that success is built upon interaction with others. Keeping this in mind, they link themselves to other people and organizations, allowing themselves to be seen and heard as they move toward success.

Goals

Now, all successful people are goal oriented in a creative way. They all have a plan, but this plan does not move in a haphazard way toward some vague desire. Instead it is a detailed and well-thought-out plan that leads to a realistic goal. First of all, they differentiate their goals into short-, intermediate-, and long-term ideas. Secondly, they never move from *A* to *Z* without taking all the intermediate steps into consideration. They are also able to adjust their plan to any given situation. Once they achieve a small success, they use it to catapult themselves into the next desired step by making their achievements known. They speak, write, lead groups, and assist others. They prefer actions that will support further actions. For instance, an actor who has faithfully mailed out his little PR cards will, after a while, contact those same casting directors requesting general interviews. Once the interview has been accomplished, he will make sure he is seen in a showcase.

In short, successful people are *used to success and expect success as they exploit success.* Once they have reached a goal, they do not sit still, but move on to the next and bigger one.

CHANGING FAILURE
INTO SUCCESS

It doesn't take a magic wand to turn failure into success. Anyone can do it. All it takes is time and effort and little steps in the right direction.

As you actively work on changing from a failure to a success profile, keep positive. Such a change cannot be achieved in a short time since you have established your negative behavior pattern a long time ago and have been conditioned to think about yourself in certain negative ways.

For the actor it might help to view acting not as your only goal, but to establish other goals as well. Looking at the profession of acting realistically, we know that only a few out of the many thousands will earn a living over the years. Most actors have to work at outside jobs.

Dr. Judith Shevren, a clinical psychologist at the Center for Counseling and Psychotherapy in Santa Monica, California, is especially interested in the problems of the creative personality.

She states, "We found that although acting was the major focus of those who felt more secure, it wasn't the only focus. They were actively engaged in doing other things. All had activities that afforded them gratification while boosting their self-esteem, such as painting, writing, real estate and other businesses outside the profession that still allowed them time for acting."*

Just having another job interest isn't enough, it's how you approach the endeavor that counts. Your soul must be fed, and your emotional need for competence and excellence must be met.

Don't demand and don't expect important successes all the time. Get used to small successes first, may these be in acting or any other related field. Get *success-prone*; expect success. Gather these successes like a bunch of sweet-smelling flowers.

As you achieve success and build goal upon goal, get used to the idea of doing *one thing at a time* and doing it well. Soon you will discover that your smaller goals will make way for more important ones.

Relax and accept the fact that once in a while we all get stuck in life. There are times that no matter how hard we push, everything seems to work against us. When this happens, do not let frustration take over, simply *fall back a little.* Do what every intelligent athlete does when he has reached a plateau, *go easy on yourself, take time, relax, and let go for a while.*

As you begin to change yourself, don't try to get rid of resentment and frustration overnight. Try just for an hour, then for a day, then for a week. Try, if only for a few minutes, to think *happy, positive thoughts.* Tell yourself in the beginning that for ten minutes at a time

I will be happy.

I will see things in a pleasant, positive way.

I will smile.

I will be tolerant.

*Richard Hoyt, Ph.D., and Judith Shevren, Ph.D., "Everything You Always Wanted to Know About Feeling Secure and Confident," *Screen Actor Magazine,* January 1979, p. 9. Copyright Screen Actors Guild, Inc., 1979.

I will like myself.

I will enjoy every moment of my life.

Get into the habit of rewarding yourself, reward yourself for a job well done, be it an interview where you were not nervous, a long session spent memorizing your lines, or the courage to make those dreaded phone calls to the agents. These rewards needn't cost you a penny. They may be listening to music, watching your favorite TV show, taking a walk, reading, or browsing through your local museum or library.

We all need *rewards*. We all need the feeling of accomplishment, the knowledge that we have done things well, the approval and applause of others.

How often have you received a compliment for a scene well done in your workshop and brushed it off as just a small thing? All of these things spell *success,* and they are successes worthy of reward. Emotionally, you must be ready for success, but this readiness involves risk. Taking risks is a major step in changing from failure to success. You must come to a point in your life and career where you have had it with failure, where you are ready to get off that Ferris wheel of frustration.

You must come to the place where you command yourself to stop, where you've had enough. It is the point of no return, and you must come to it before you can truly change your behavior pattern. Once you have reached this point, the road to success is open to you. Go after success, you deserve it. Granted, it's not always easy, but nothing in life that is really worth-while is easy. Failure is easy, you just don't do anything.

CONCLUSION

This brings us to the end of the book and as such to the end of the road we have traveled together. I hope *The Actor's Survival Guide for Today's Film Industry* has been helpful in guiding your first steps in an acting career. I hope it has made things clearer and easier. Some of you, after reading what I have said, may question the wisdom of choosing acting for a career, yet you may still want to be a part of this exciting industry. Forge ahead. There are numerous satisfying careers to be made in casting, agenting, and producing.

I believe that we artists who work in this industry have been especially blessed. We express thoughts and feelings, and at times we bring a beauty to the screen that makes for a better understanding of humanity. From this point of view, every day we take part in the Lord's divine creation.

You are going out into a profession that will, because of its complexity, bring you joy as well as sorrow. As you go, always remember:

Know what you are doing.
Enjoy what you are doing.
Do it well.

May the Lord and Creator of all art be with you on your road to success.

INDEX